Character Design for Beginners

MANGA TECHNIQUES

Vol.4

An Instruction Manual for Manga Artists Around the World

MANGA TECHNIQUES Vol. 4
Character Design for Beginners

Copyright © 2003 S.E.Inc

First published in 2003 by S.E.Inc.
1-20-60 Miyauchi, Nakahara-ku, Kawasaki City 211-0051, Japan

Editing : Shunji Haraguchi
Illustrations : Kai Hinomoto
Himura Enji
Mitsuki Michitaka
Mai Yamaki

Distributor
Japan Publications Trading Co, Ltd.
1-2-1 Sarugaku-cho, Chiyoda-ku, Tokyo 101-0064, Japan
E-mail : jpt@jptco.co.jp
URL : http://www.jptco.co.jp/

First printing : February 2003

ISBN 4-88996-111-9
Printed in Japan

CONTENTS

Character Design for Beginners

Chapter 1 : Before You Begin Drawing   05

What Kind of Characters Do You Like?   06

The Key to Creating Characters   07

Creating Friendly Characters   08

Basic Character Representation 1   Knowing Your Style   09

Basic Character Representation 2   Basic Proportion   14

Basic Character Representation 3   17
Creating Characters Using Patterns

Basic Character Representation 4   22
Elaborating, Transforming and Bending

Chapter 2 : Drawing the Face, Hands and Legs   27

Basics for Drawing the Face 1

   Drawing Faces of Male, Female and Children   28

   Using Rotation   29

   Using Patterns   The Face   30

   Facial Representation Samples   31

Basics for Drawing the Face 2

   Characteristics of Different Facial Shapes   32

   Changing the Shapes of Eyes, Nose, Mouth and Hair   33

   Exaggeration of Facial Shapes   34

Drawing the Eyes   35

Exaggeration of the Eyes and Using Patterns   36

Drawing the Nose and Mouth   37

Representation Samples for the Eyes   38

Alternating Facial Expressions   40

Samples of Facial Angles and Expressions Using the Eyes   41

Drawing the Hair   42

Drawing the Hands   44

Drawing the Feet   46

Chapter 3 : Drawing the Whole Body   49

A: Creating Realistic Full-Figure Style Characters   50

   The Drawing Process   51

   Character Chart   52

   Creating Two Characters by Changing Head-Torso Scale   53

   Character Chart -- Young Male and Boy   54

   Drawing Characters with Tools/Objects   56

B: Drawing Fine-Line Sketch Style Characters   57

   Game Design Type Characters   58

   Normal Type Characters   59

   Fighting Type Characters   60

C: Drawing Simplified Anime Style Characters   62

   Developing Characters Using Patterns   63

   Drawing 5 Head-Lengthed Characters   64

   Drawing 7 Head-Lengthed Characters   65

   Drawing 10 Head-Lengthed Characters   66

Chapter 4 : Moving the Characters   67

Realistic Full-Figure Style Characters -- Sitting Poses 1   68

Realistic Full-Figure Style Characters -- Sitting Poses 2   69

Realistic Full-Figure Style Characters -- Sitting Poses 3   70

Realistic Full-Figure Style Characters -- Running Poses   71

Simplified Anime Style Characters -- Running Poses   72

Simplified Anime Style Characters -- Miscellaneous Poses   73

Fine-Line Sketch Style Characters -- Miscellaneous Poses   74

Fine-Line Sketch Style Characters -- Running Poses   75

Fine-Line Sketch Style Characters -- Leg and Back Poses   76

Fine-Line Sketch Style Characters --   77

           Samples of Putting in Outlines

Samples   78

Samples   79

Samples   80

Chapter 1

Before You Begin Drawing

To create *manga* characters, you need to know the basic structure of the human body in addition to having basic sketching skills. Most importantly, however, you need to have the techniques to adequately express each character's traits. So, before you actually begin creating characters, you should know some of the basics of creating characters.

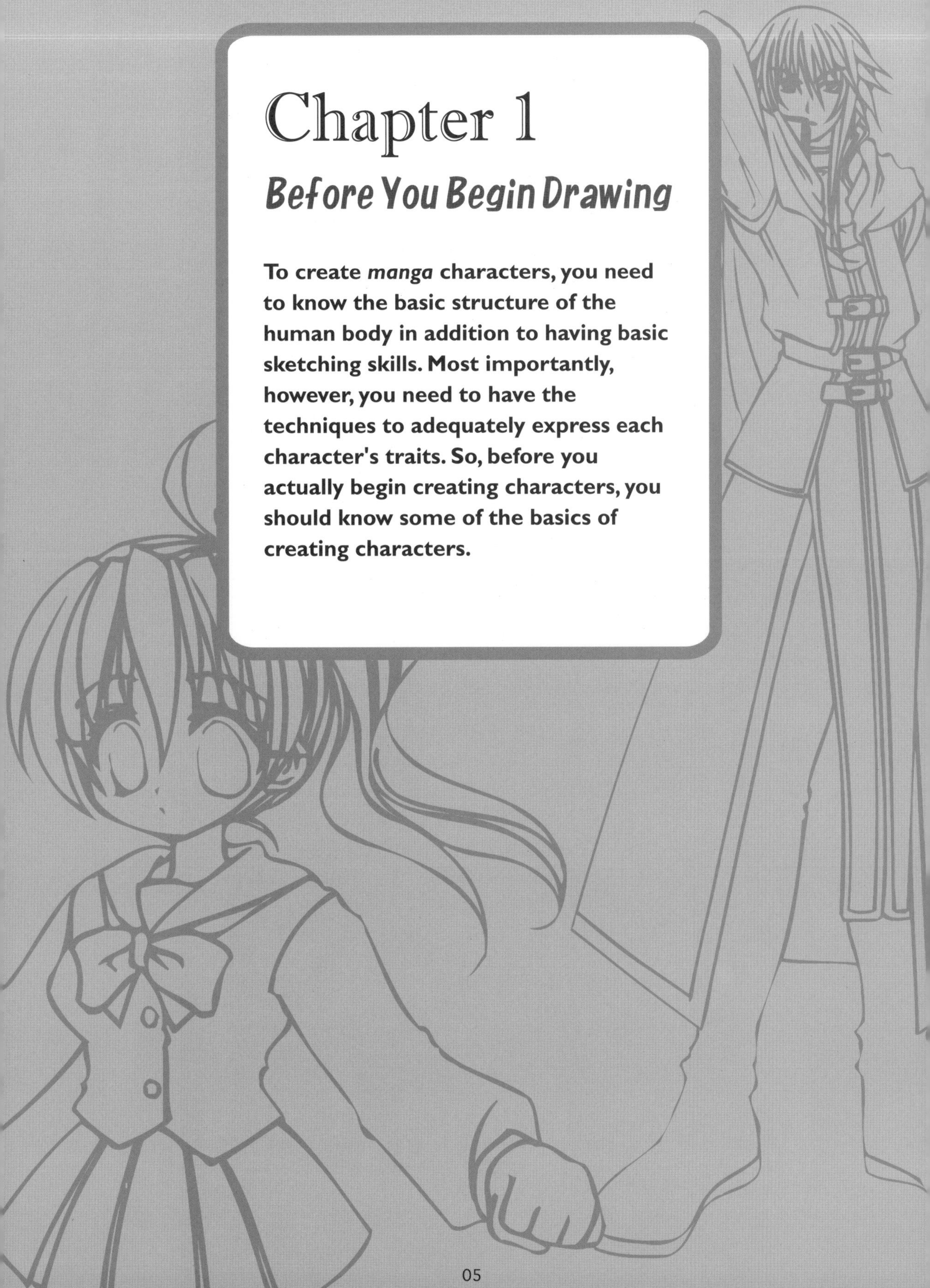

What Kind of Characters Do You Like?

Type A

Well-balanced realistic full-figure style characters with thick lines and good balance

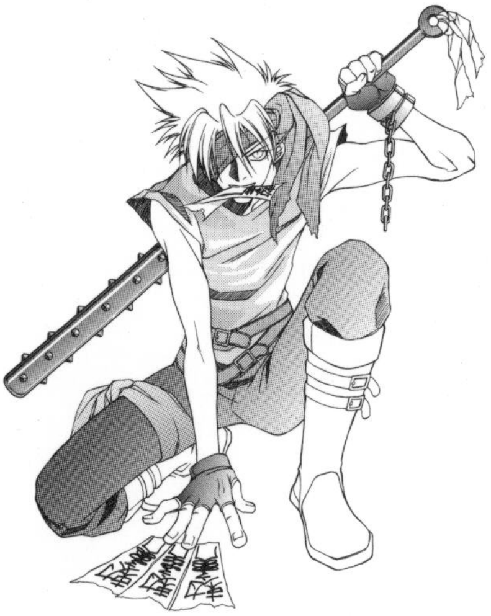

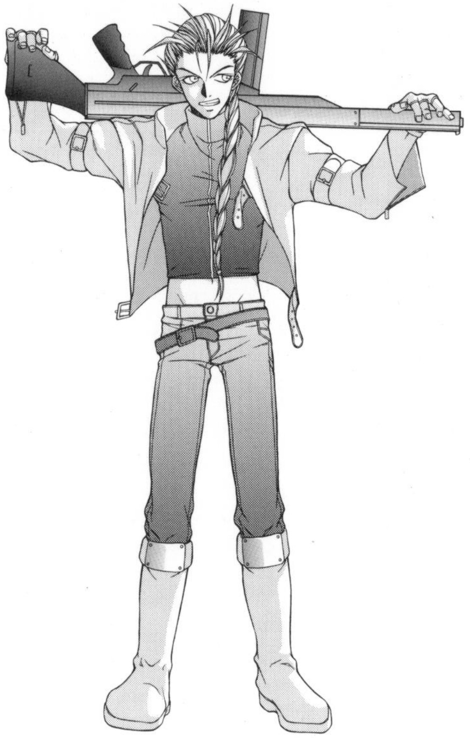

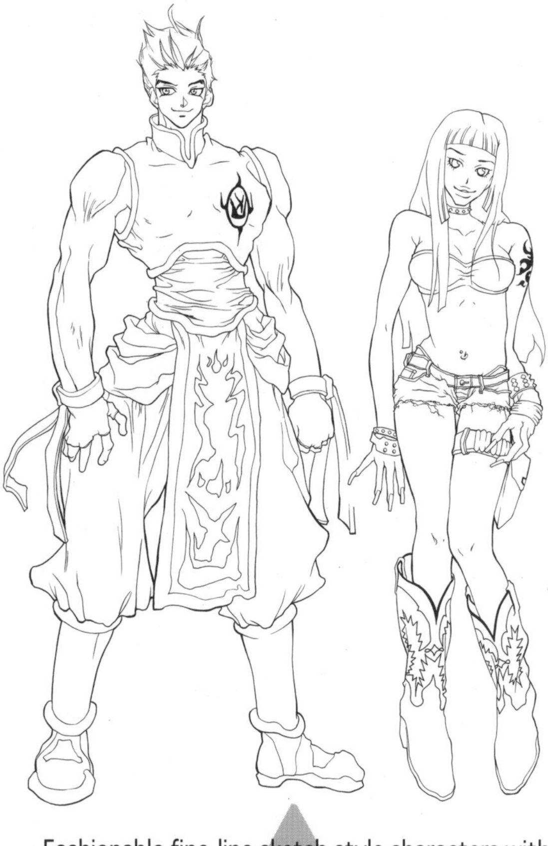

Fashionable fine-line sketch style characters with vivid lines

Type B

Type C

Simplified anime style characters with few details

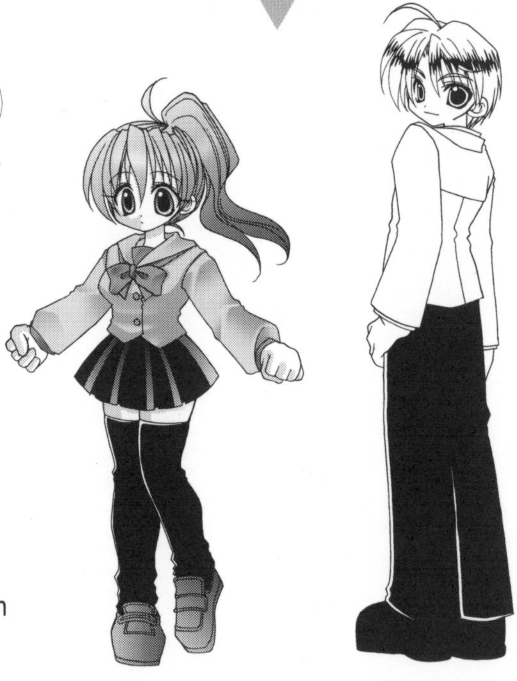

The Key to Creating Characters

It is quite difficult to create characters with only your imagination to aid you. But it will become much easier if you use a guideline to create them.

Create a figure and change or add detail to create different characters (making patterns.) You can create variety of characters by making a rough sketch of a figure and alternating its height and gender.

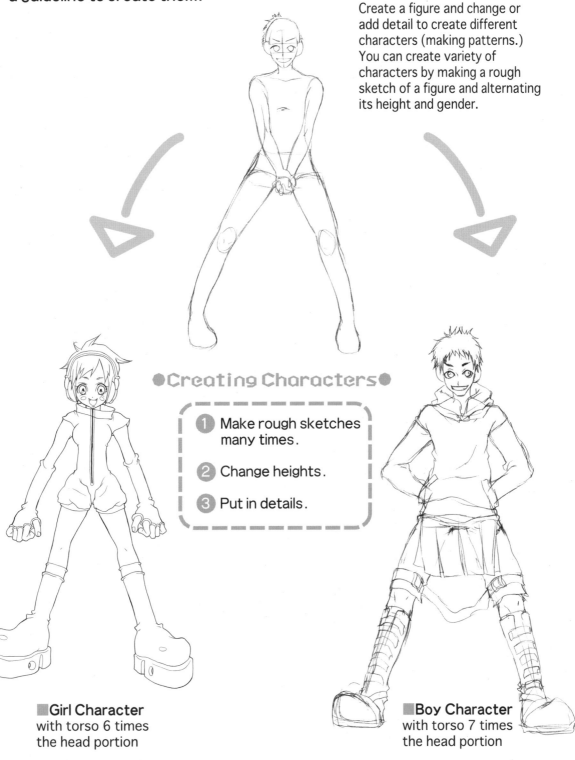

●Creating Characters●

1. Make rough sketches many times.
2. Change heights.
3. Put in details.

■Girl Character
with torso 6 times the head portion

■Boy Character
with torso 7 times the head portion

Creating Friendly Characters

One of the most important thing about character-making is to make the characters look friendly and lovable. You can do this by having them wear fashionable clothing, adding small details to bring out their personality, or having them pose attractively. Who would want to buy comics if all the characters were standing lifelessly wearing terrible clothes, right?

■Adding cat ears and tails makes characters look cute.

■Having good taste in clothing is important.

■Poses compliment character's ideal body form.

■Changing hair styles and adding small items are very useful in *manga*-making.

Basic Character Representation 1

Knowing Your Style

○ What kind of characters would seem interesting?

Below are three completely different types of characters. They are drawn by three *manga*-writers who use different styles. It might be a good idea to use their techniques as examples to find and become good at drawing *manga* in your own favorite way.

A: Realistic Full-Figure Style

A: Creating realistic full-figure style characters involves using sketches of human body as a base and then develops them into *manga* characters. Having sketching skills is very important in using this style.

B: Fine-line Sketch Style

B: When creating fine-line sketch characters, using composition is not important. This style is more like a fashion design that you can start drawing from any place using tiny strokes. Thus, this style is often used by professionals or by complete beginners. Although this style may not be the perfect style to create balanced figures, it enables to exaggerate and elaborate on each character's traits and thus making it look interesting.

C: Simplified Anime Style

C: When drawing characters in simplified anime style, sketches of human body are not necessary. Instead, you can use simple figures as examples, like sketches of models of human body. As long as you understand the basic structure and how the joints work, this style can become very useful because you can disregard muscles and other small details.

A: Let's Draw

Realistic Full-Figure Style Characters

Let's draw a masculine male character (although let's avoid those S.F. style machos.) First, make a rough sketch and then build it by adding details, small and big. You should also try drawing sitting and moving poses.

The Sketching Process

1

Make a rough sketch of a body including muscle tones.

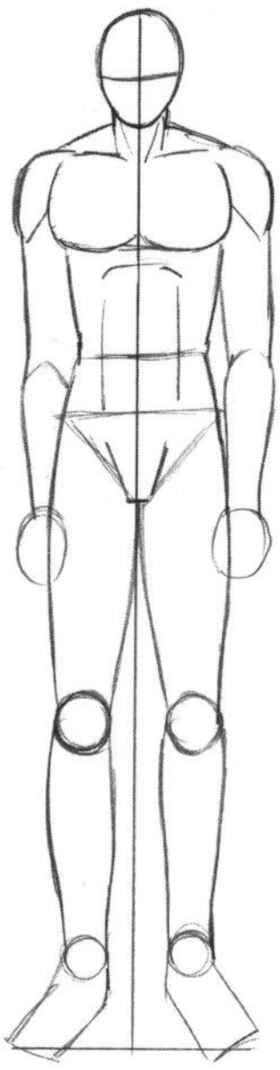

2

Add hair and shorts.

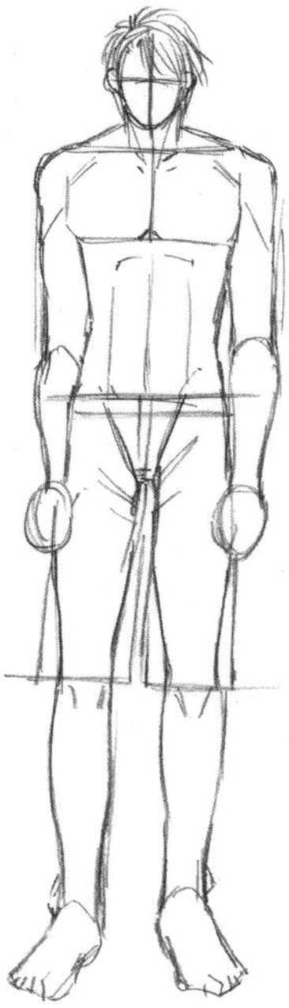

3

Clean the lines and finish.

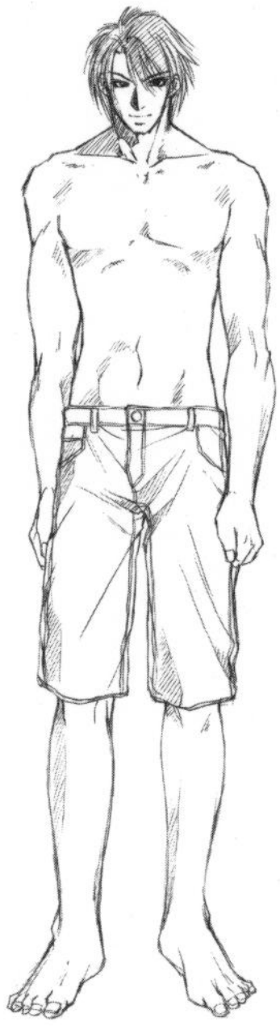

Moving Pose

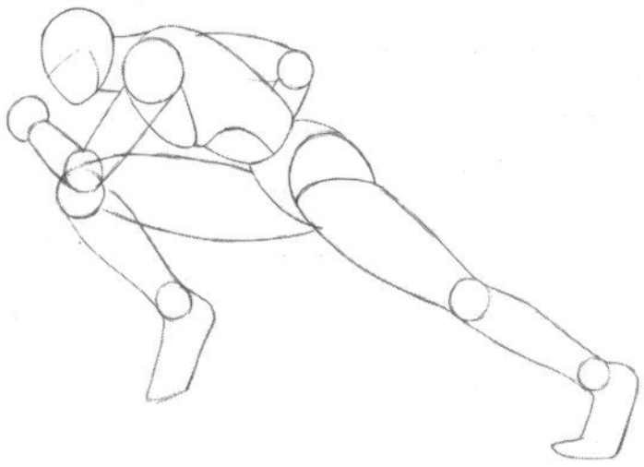

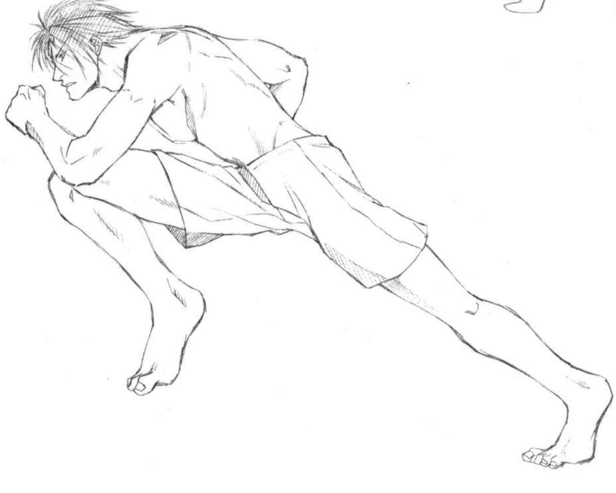

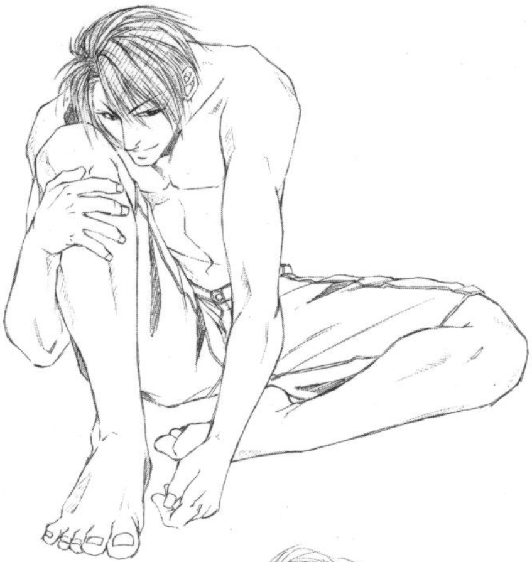

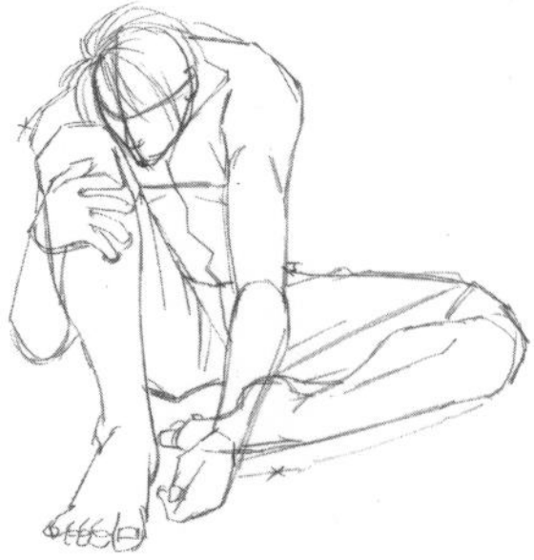

B: Let's Draw

Fine-line Sketch Style Characters

Unlike the photographic and proportional realistic full-figure characters, fine-line sketch style characters rely on vivid and dynamic lines (the foundation of this style is that you sketch human bodies using these lines.)

The down side of this style is that you need to have basic sketching skills in order to create balanced characters. However, this style will enable you to create colorful and lively characters just by adding in small details. The best way is to draw a single detail over and over again with long and constant lines.

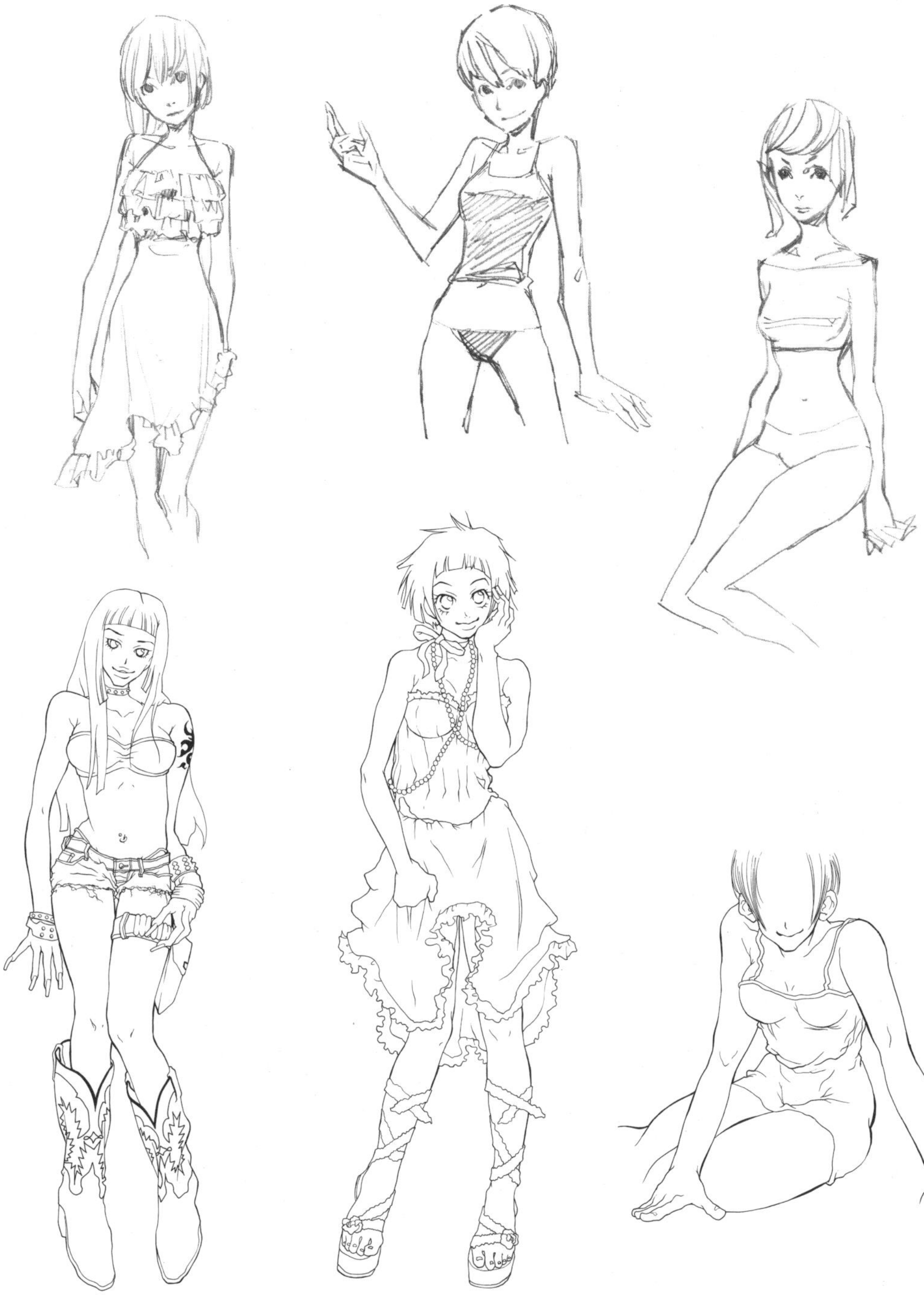

C: Let's Draw

Simplified Anime Style Characters

There is a model of the human body created using simple cubes. Simplified anime style characters are often created by sketching simple outlines of this model, posing in many different ways.
The key is to ignore the muscle tones and complicated details, and drawing it very simply.
By simplifying complex movements, the characters would win kids' hearts.

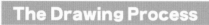

The Drawing Process

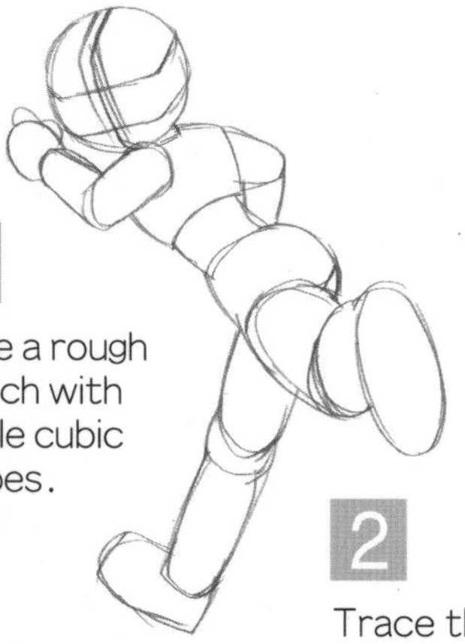

1

Make a rough sketch with simple cubic shapes.

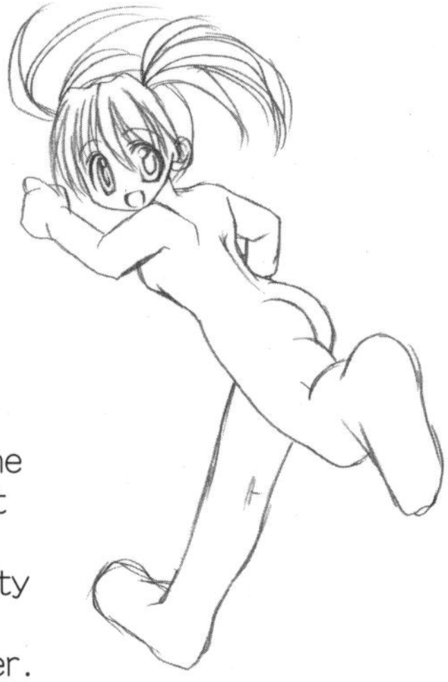

2

Trace the lines that suit the personality of the character.

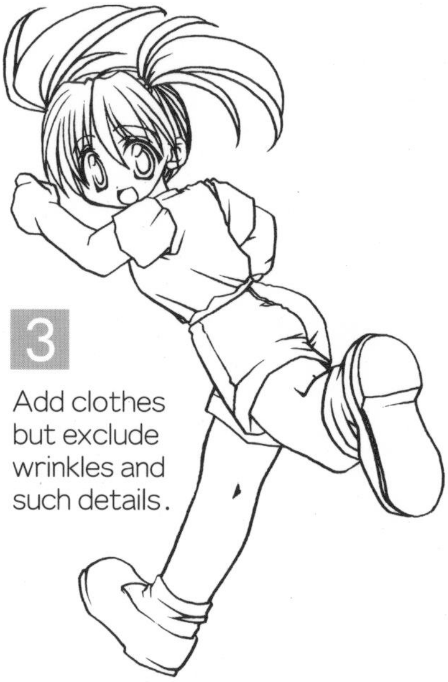

3

Add clothes but exclude wrinkles and such details.

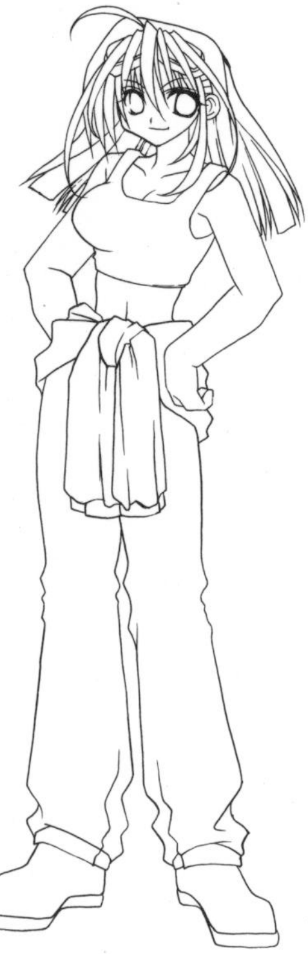

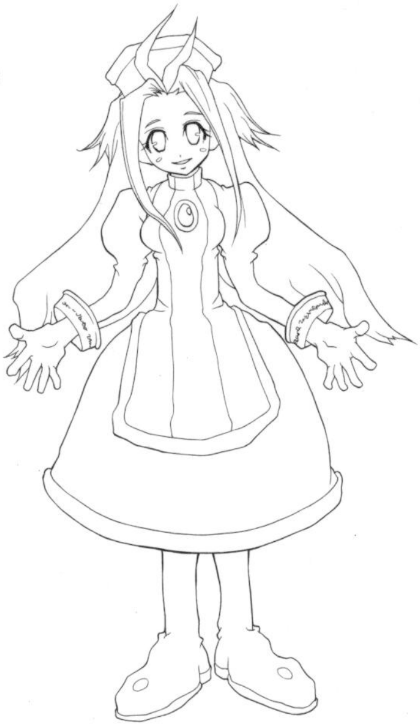

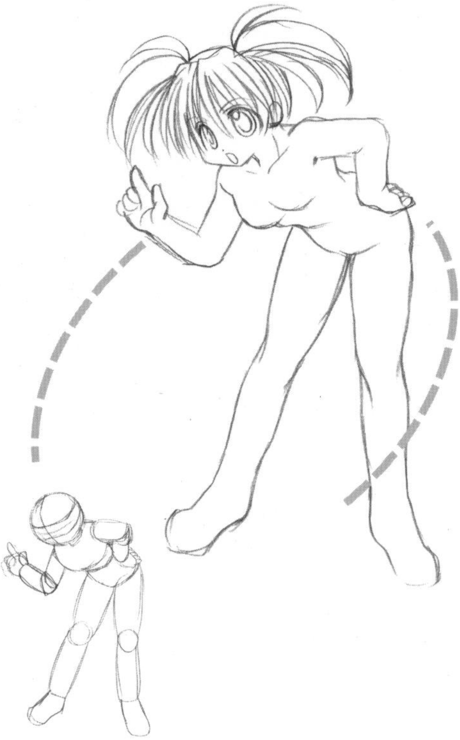

Did You Find "Your" Style?

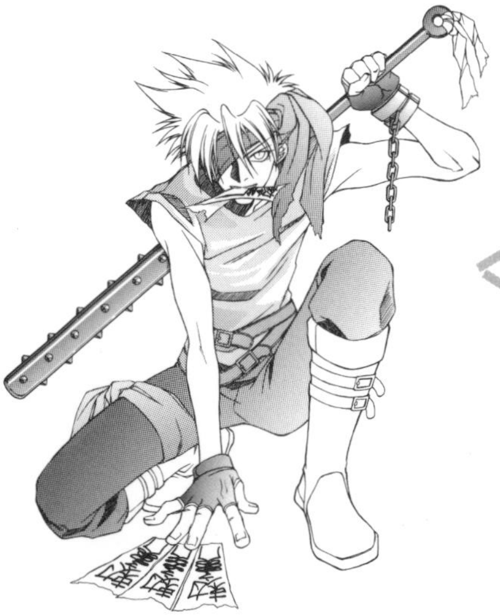

Realistic Full-figure Type

Realistic characters are usually seen in *manga* based on real life.
These *manga* anticipate dynamic story development.

Fine-line Sketch Type

Any kind of *manga*, from S.F. to domestic drama, seems possible with these graphic but original, simply-sketched characters. How would you cast them?

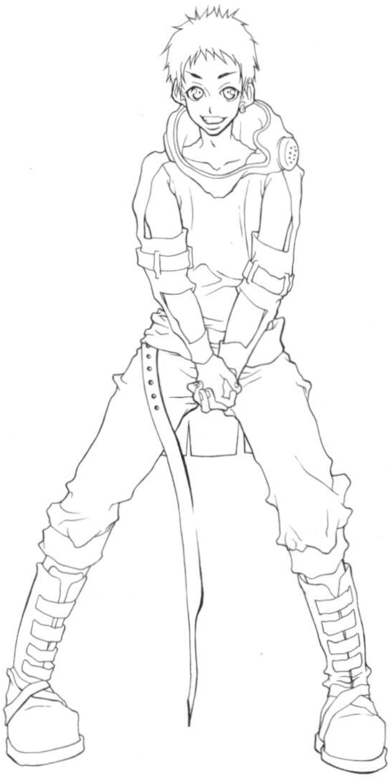

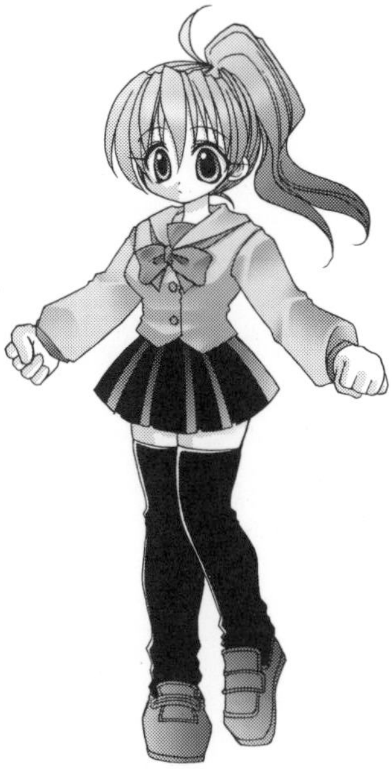

Simplified Anime Type

This style is often used in *manga* for children, games, and anime. Simplified limbs and details make these characters suitable for *manga* with straightforward storylines.

Have you found the style that suits your taste? Have you found the style that compliments your technique? Keep searching for your style and proceed while understanding the basics of character-making.

Basic Character Representation 2

Understanding the Basic Structure of the Human Body

These are models that show basic human features. Use a doll in the pictures and begin drawing.

Basic Proportion

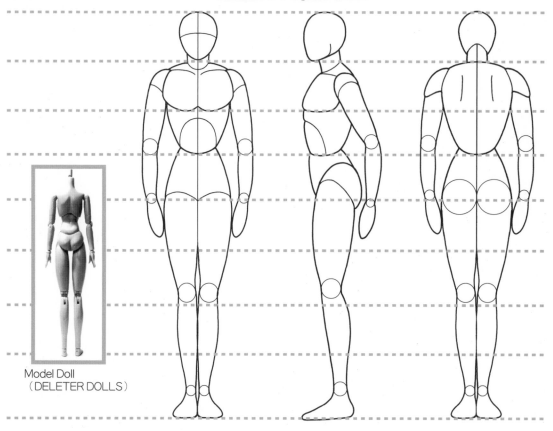

Model Doll
（DELETER DOLLS）

When drawing either male and female, remember that the bodies of male and female differ substantially in build.

Different Ways to Draw Male and Female Body Parts

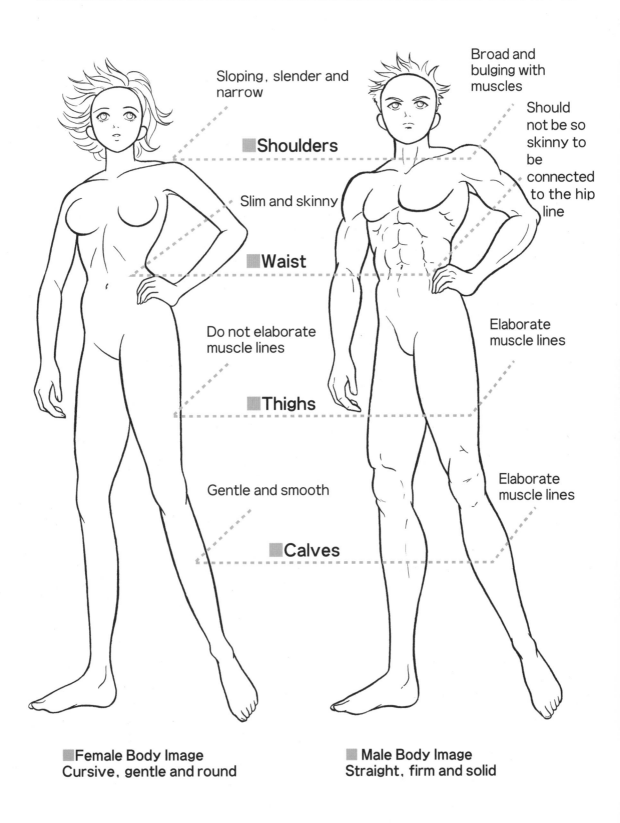

Sloping, slender and narrow

Broad and bulging with muscles

■Shoulders

Should not be so skinny to be connected to the hip line

Slim and skinny

■Waist

Do not elaborate muscle lines

Elaborate muscle lines

■Thighs

Gentle and smooth

Elaborate muscle lines

■Calves

■Female Body Image
Cursive, gentle and round

■ Male Body Image
Straight, firm and solid

15

Capturing the Subject Three - Dimensionally

There are some important details and joints that you should remember when drawing characters.

■The shoulder is not perpendicular to the neck.

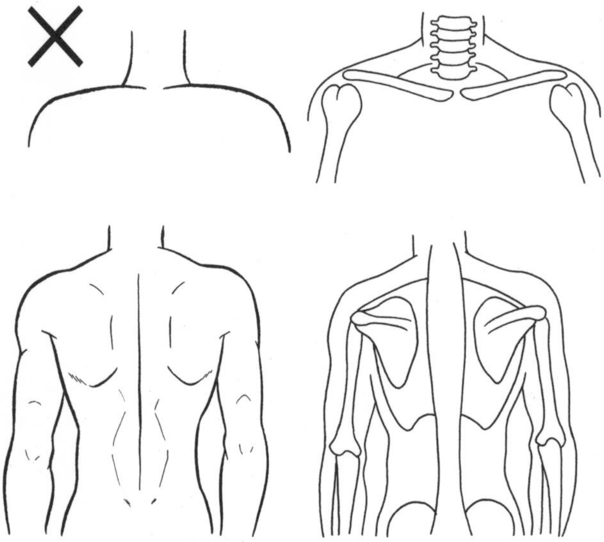

■Hip

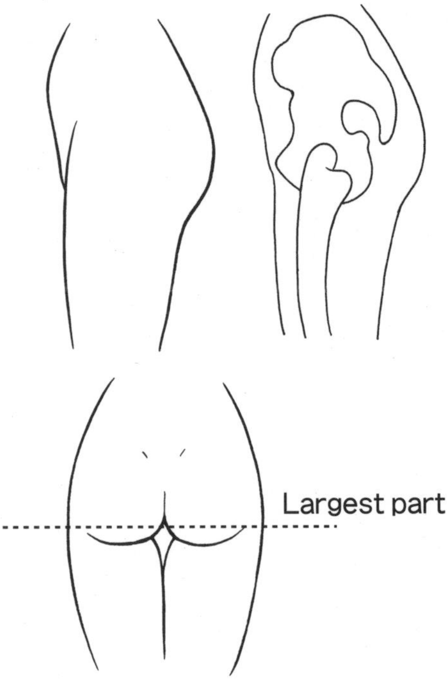
Largest part

Size Ratio of Different Parts

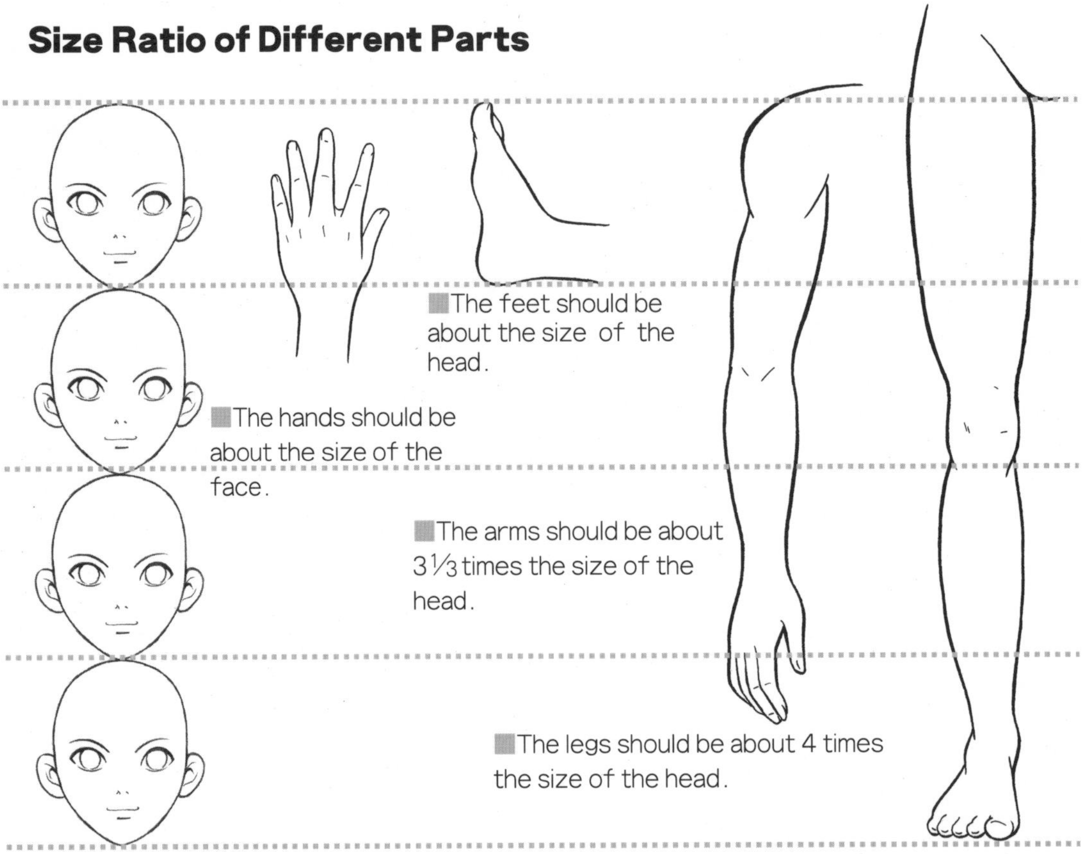

■The feet should be about the size of the head.

■The hands should be about the size of the face.

■The arms should be about 3⅓ times the size of the head.

■The legs should be about 4 times the size of the head.

Basic Character Representation 3

Using Patterns to Create Different Characters

Several characters appear in a same story. Let's try to create different characters using a single original and making patterns.

 Anyone can draw one or two characters, but writing story-based *manga* involves drawing tens, or sometimes hundreds, of different side-kicks and enemies. In these kinds of situations, being able to use patterns becomes very important.

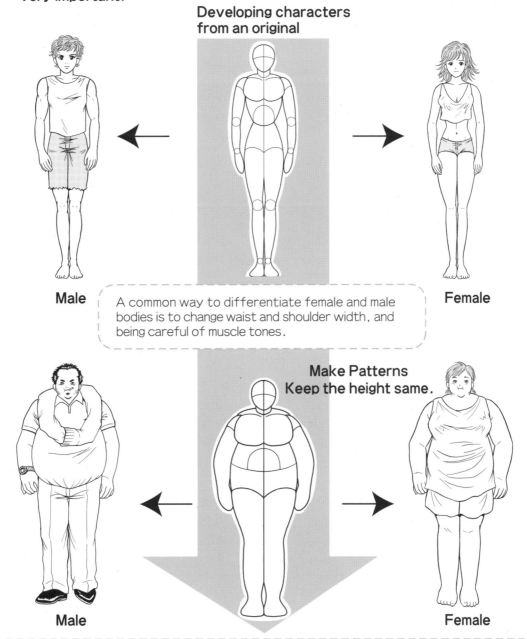

Developing characters from an original

Male

Female

A common way to differentiate female and male bodies is to change waist and shoulder width, and being careful of muscle tones.

Make Patterns
Keep the height same.

Male

Female

The build of large characters are often times similar, but you can distinguish each of them by changing the size of the chest, hands and feet.

Samples of Developing Characters Using Patterns

Whatever style it you use, the characters will seem somewhat similar in one way or another if they are drawn by the same person. Use the pattern technique to vary your characters.

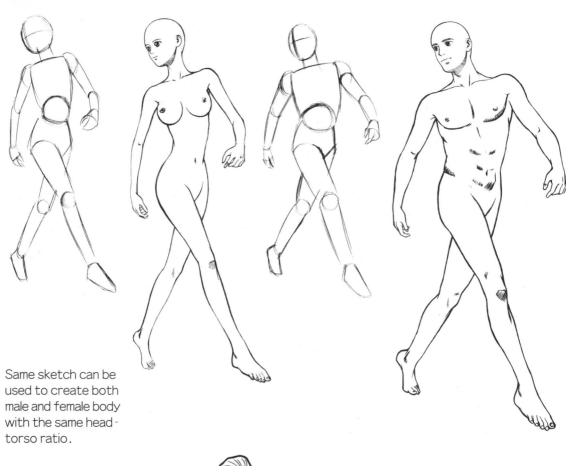

Same sketch can be used to create both male and female body with the same head-torso ratio.

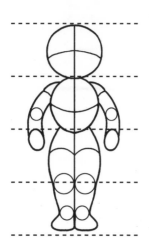

Considering the head as one unit, this sketch of 4 head-length body can be used to draw both an old man and a boy.

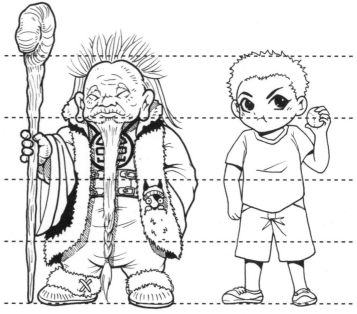

Creating 3 Characters Changing the Head - Torso Proportion

The size of the head stays the same. Using this same head (circle) and considering it as one unit, you can create three different characters with 5, 7 and 10 head-lenghed bodies.

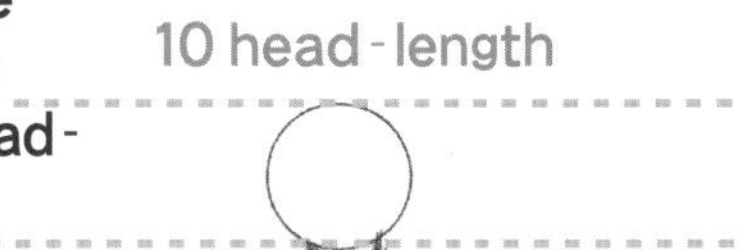
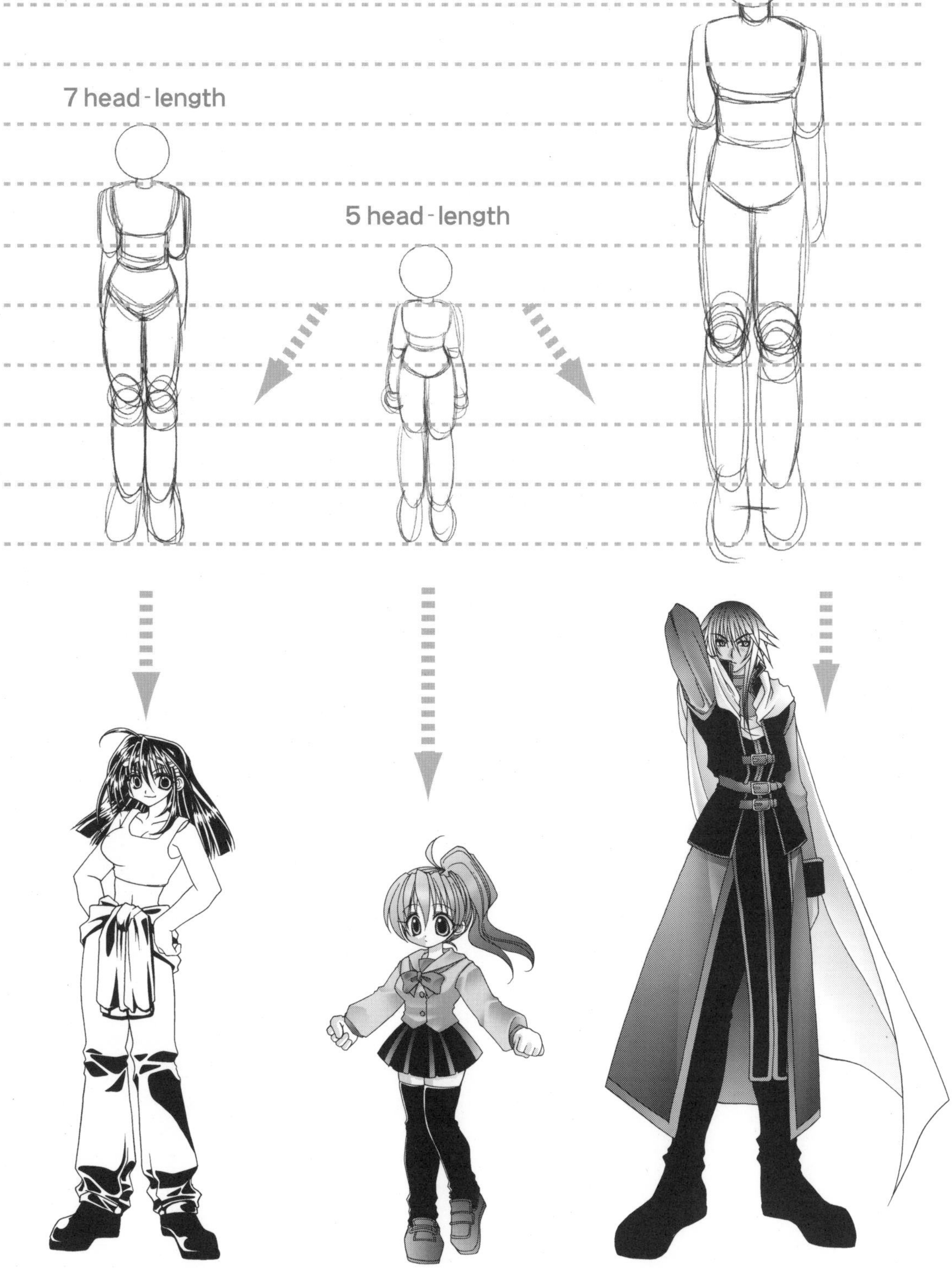
10 head - length
7 head - length
5 head - length

The size of the head looks much bigger for the 5 head - lengthed than the 10 head - lengthed body.

Realistic Portrayals and Appropriating Them for Manga Characters

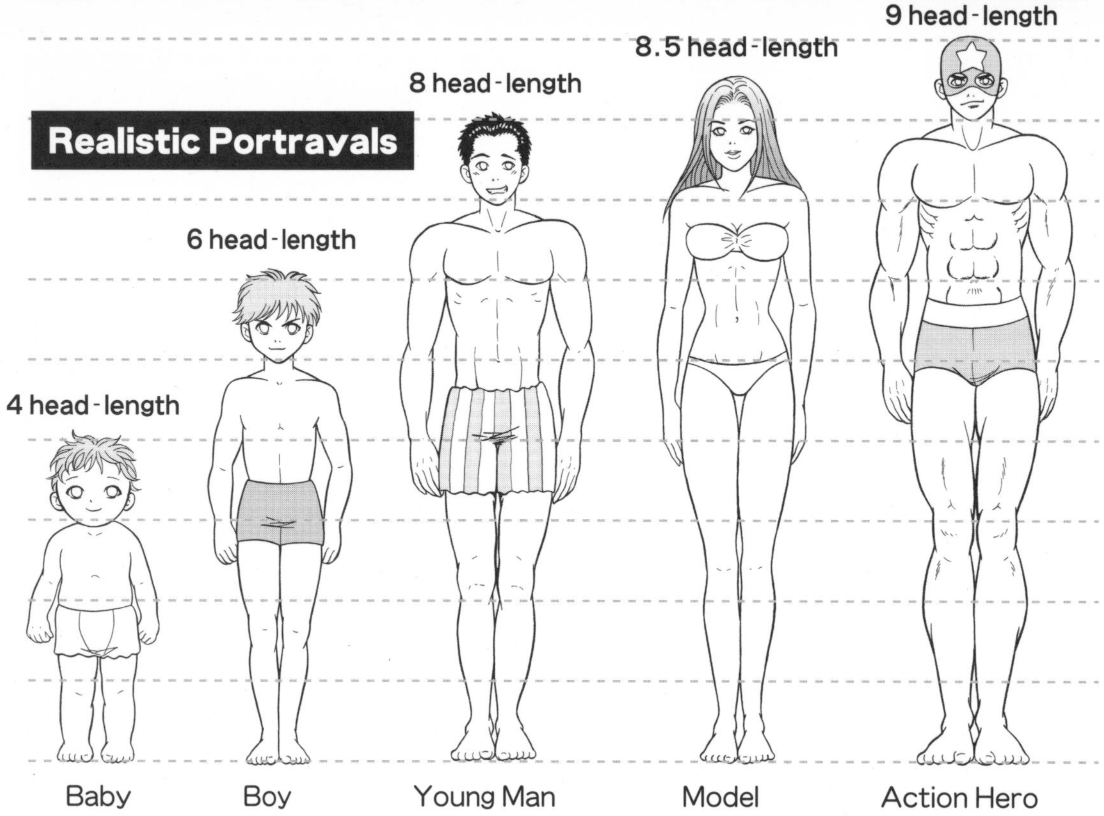

Realistic Portrayals
4 head-length
6 head-length
8 head-length
8.5 head-length
9 head-length
Baby
Boy
Young Man
Model
Action Hero

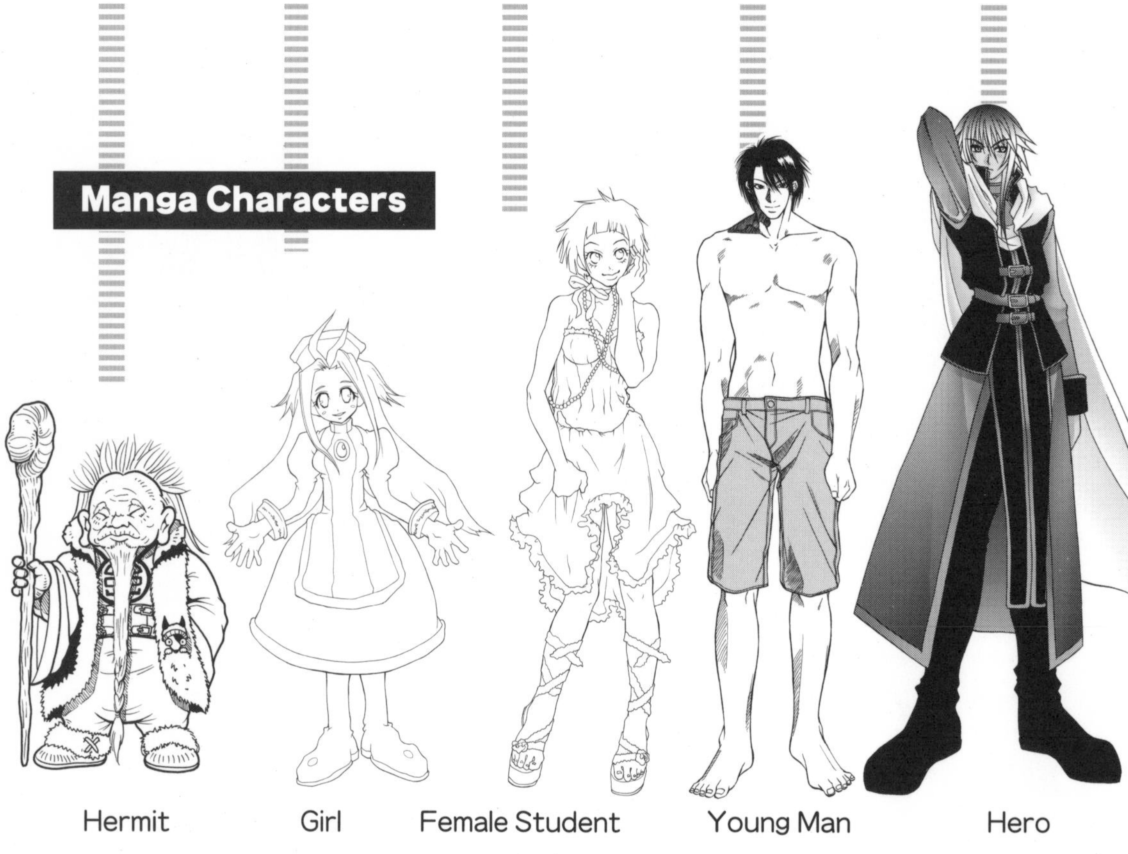

Manga Characters
Hermit
Girl
Female Student
Young Man
Hero

Samples of Characters Created by Using Patterns

First, create an original without putting in small details like nose and mouth. (Although these characters are facing forward, you should also create originals facing sideways and backwards.)

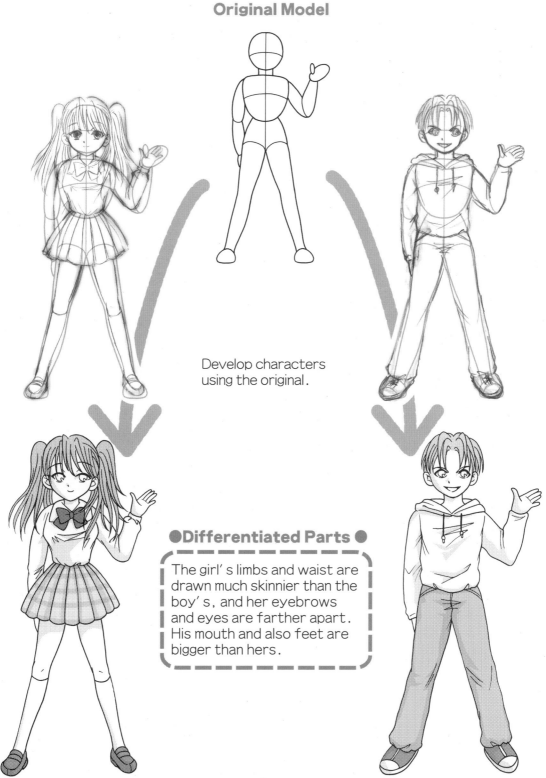

Original Model

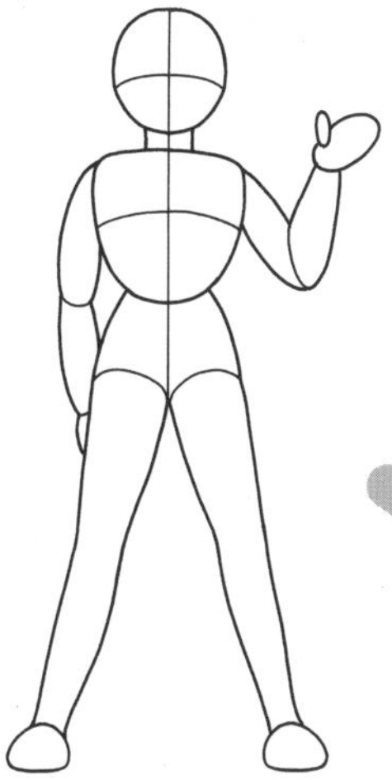

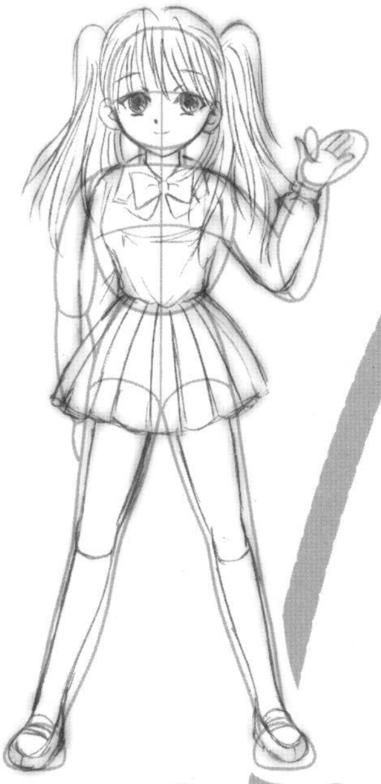

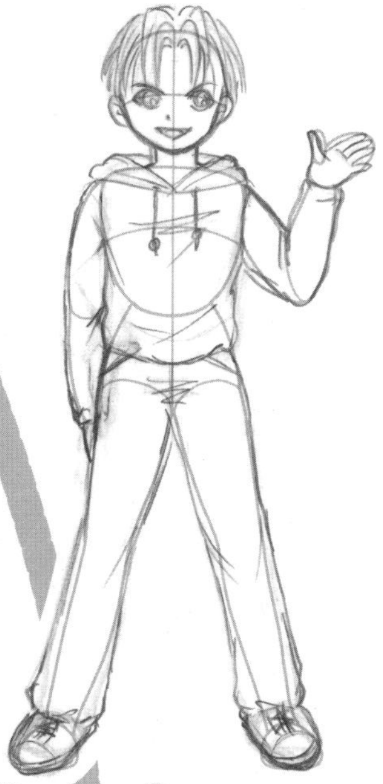

Develop characters using the original.

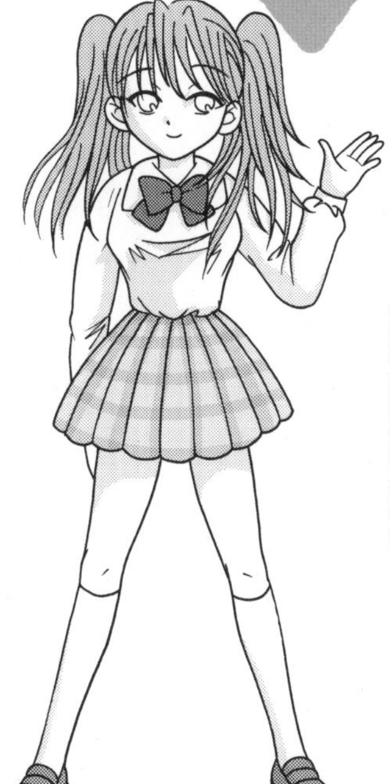

●Differentiated Parts●

The girl's limbs and waist are drawn much skinnier than the boy's, and her eyebrows and eyes are farther apart. His mouth and also feet are bigger than hers.

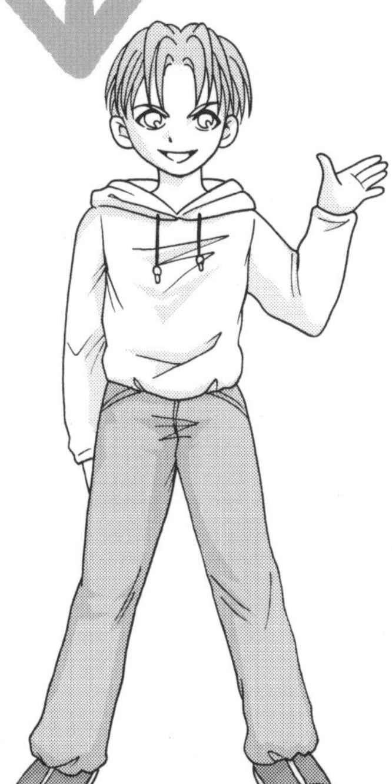

Basic Character Representation 4

Techniques to Elaborate, Transform and Bend

To bring out each character's personalities, you should be able to elaborate, transform and bend each representation in addition to having good sketching skills.

Look at the two pictures below.

Photographic representation

Elaborated representation

A
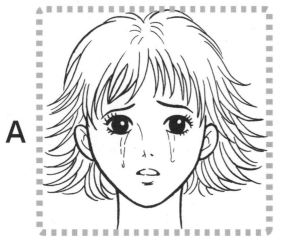

Mouth is drawn bigger than it actually is and the tears are coming down like a waterfall.

Photographic representation

Elaborated representation

B

Eyebrows form large curves and the mouth is bigger than her facial outline.

How to Use Exaggeration

Making a *manga* with a child character as the protagonist can be tricky. You should pay careful attention of the balance of the narrow torso and the long limbs.

●Sample of a Game Character●

Characters that appear in games have very simple and mobile forms. The outline of both face and body is usually symbolized.

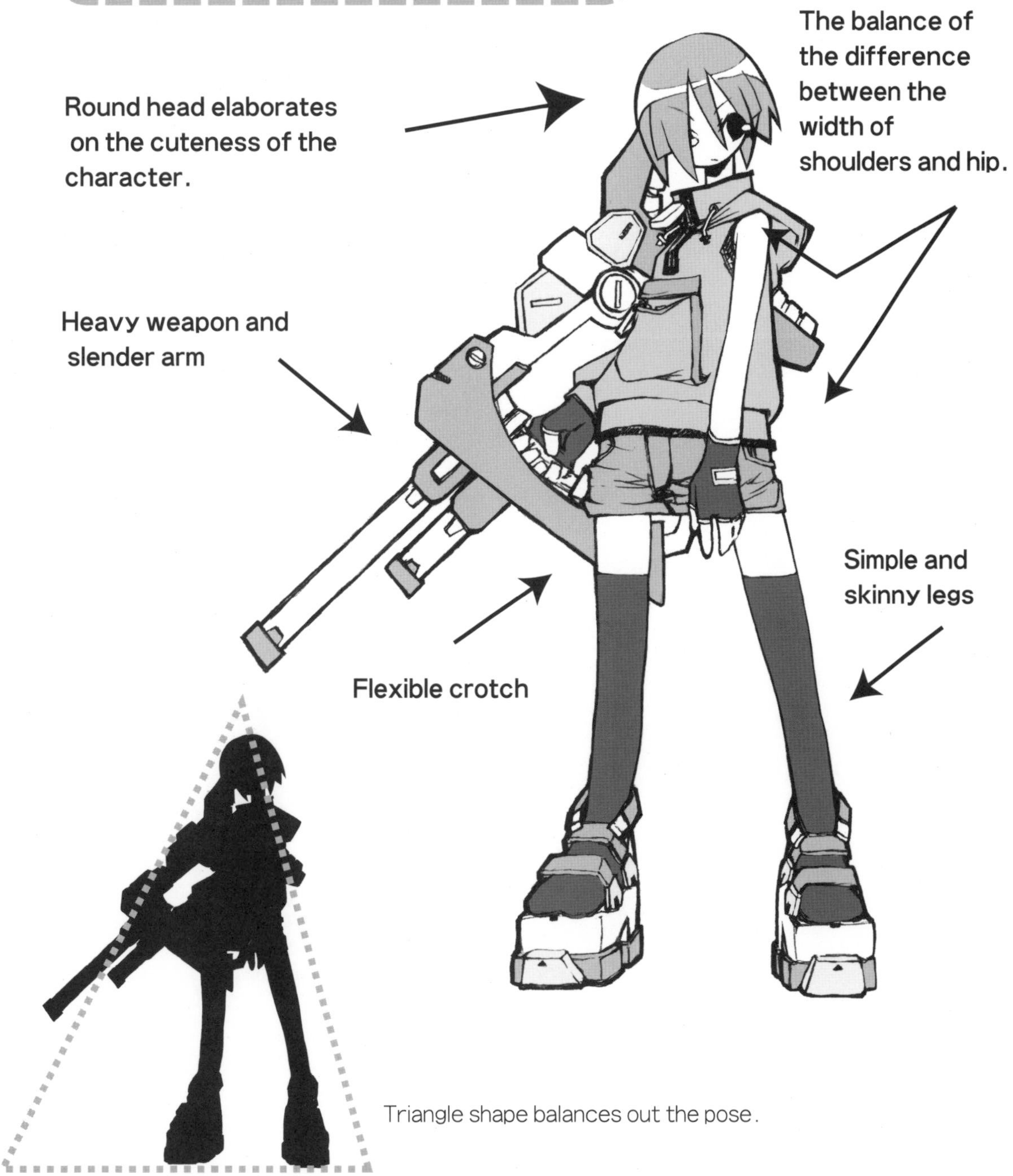
The balance of the difference between the width of shoulders and hip.
Round head elaborates on the cuteness of the character.
Heavy weapon and slender arm
Simple and skinny legs
Flexible crotch

Triangle shape balances out the pose.

Samples of Exaggeration Using Angles

A character with even an average height can seem impressive if you use angled exaggeration and right frame representation.

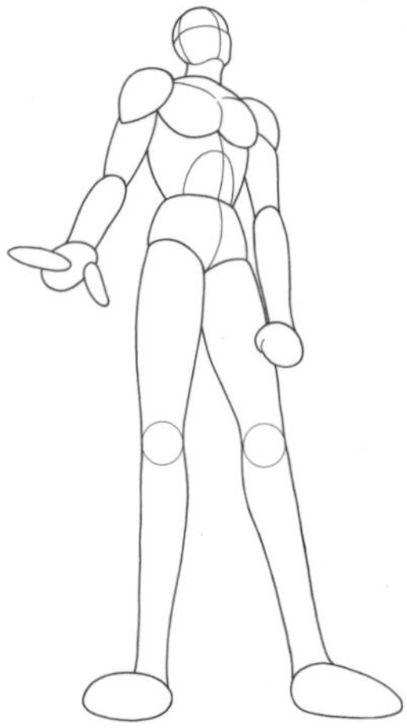

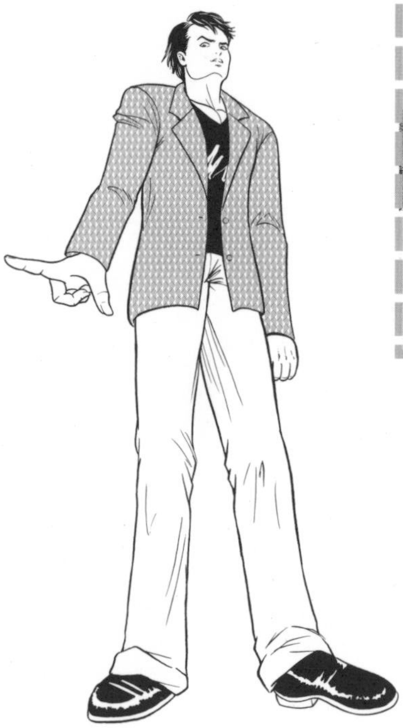

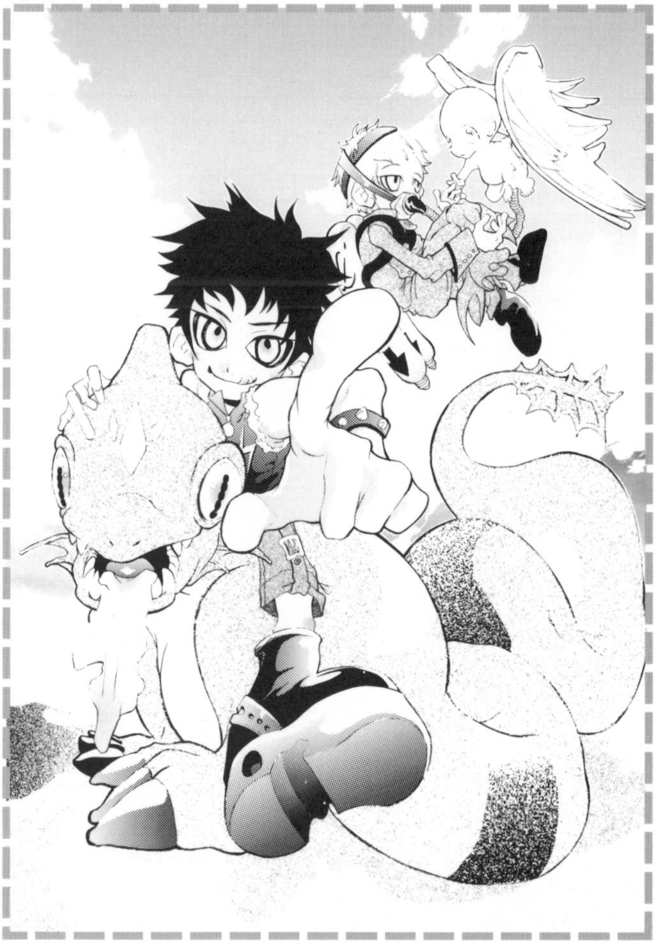

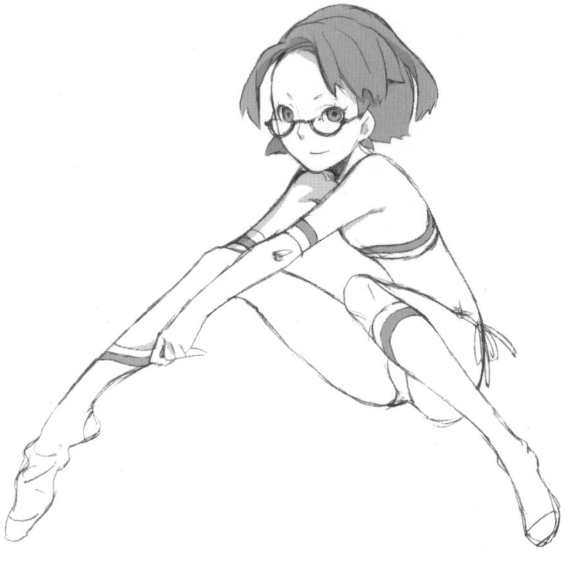

Samples of Exaggeration of Different Body Parts

Let' s look at the exaggerated parts of this 3 head-lengthed character.

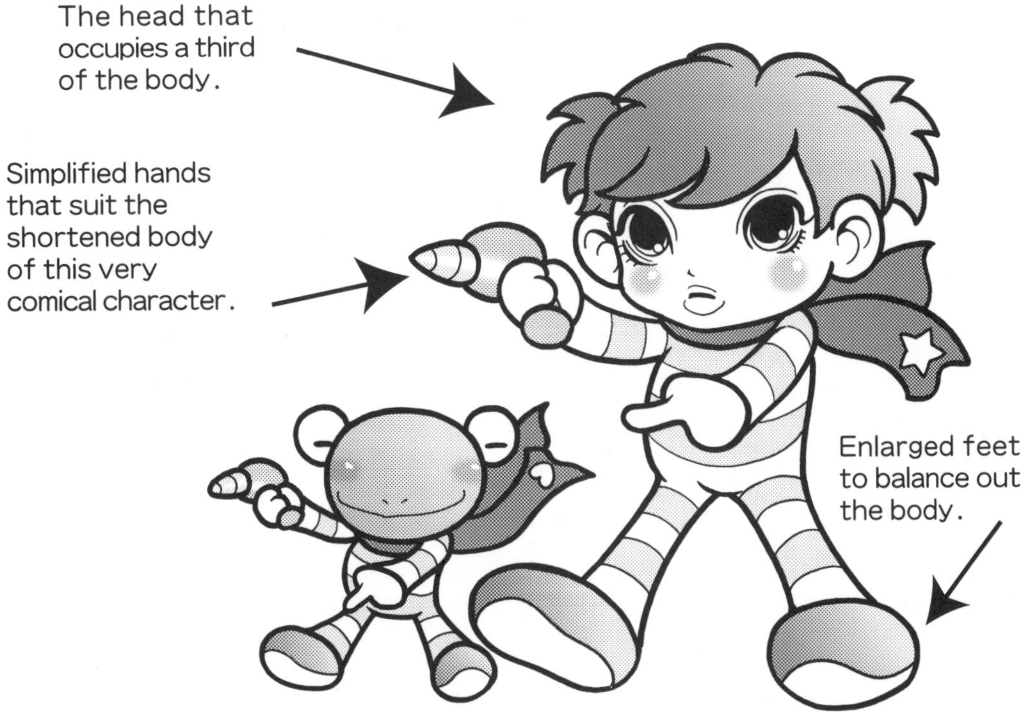
The head that occupies a third of the body.
Simplified hands that suit the shortened body of this very comical character.
Enlarged feet to balance out the body.

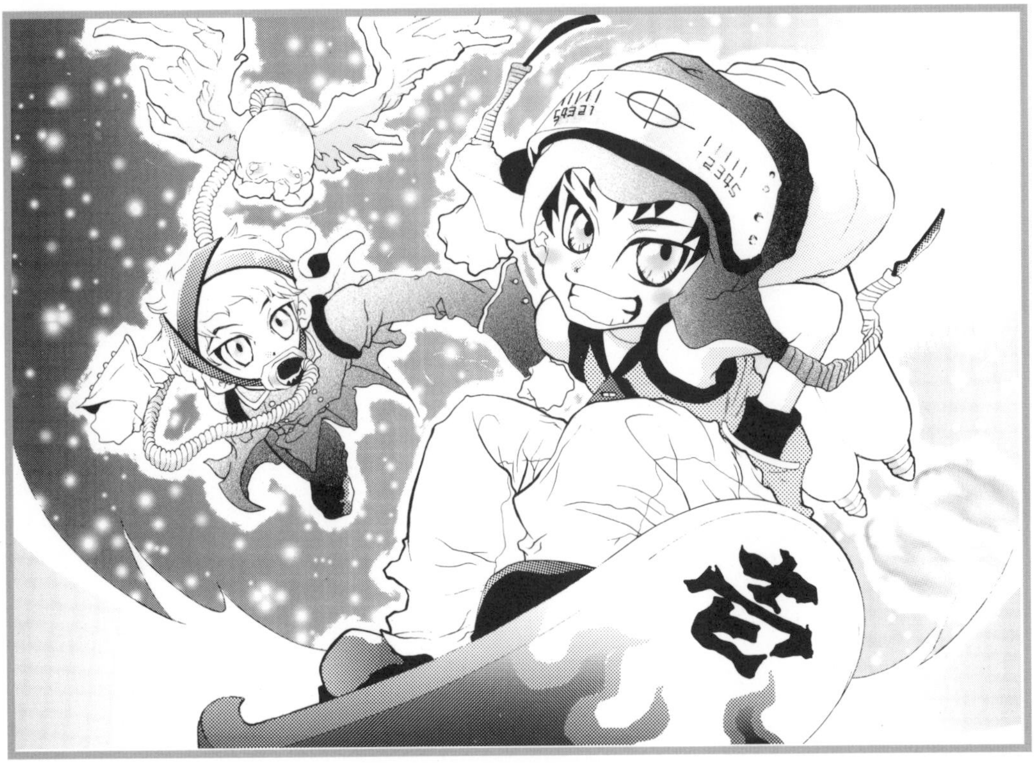

Decoration (Gothic)

A little different from exaggeration, decoration involves personifying (or making them look like cats) characters by adding cat ears and tails. Using this technique you can create adorable pet characters. You can also have them pose like real animals.

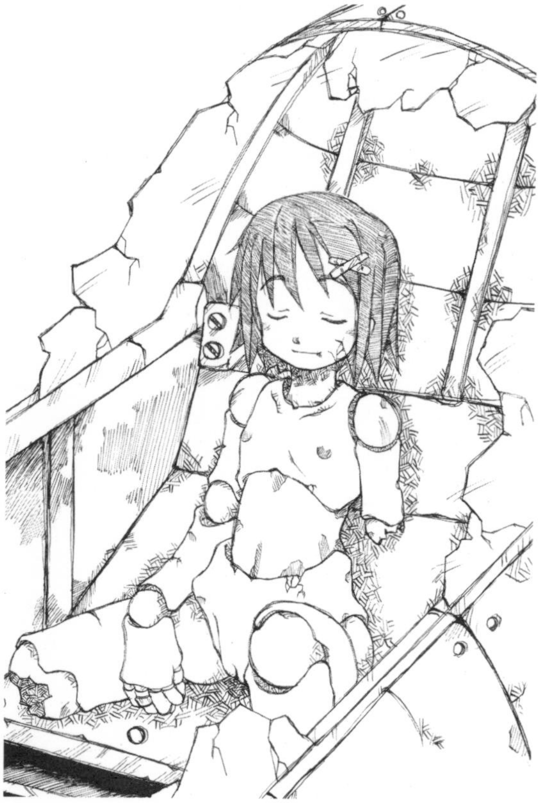

Anything is possible in the world of *manga*.
Stretch your imagination beyond common sense and come up with a character like this: a lifeless doll.

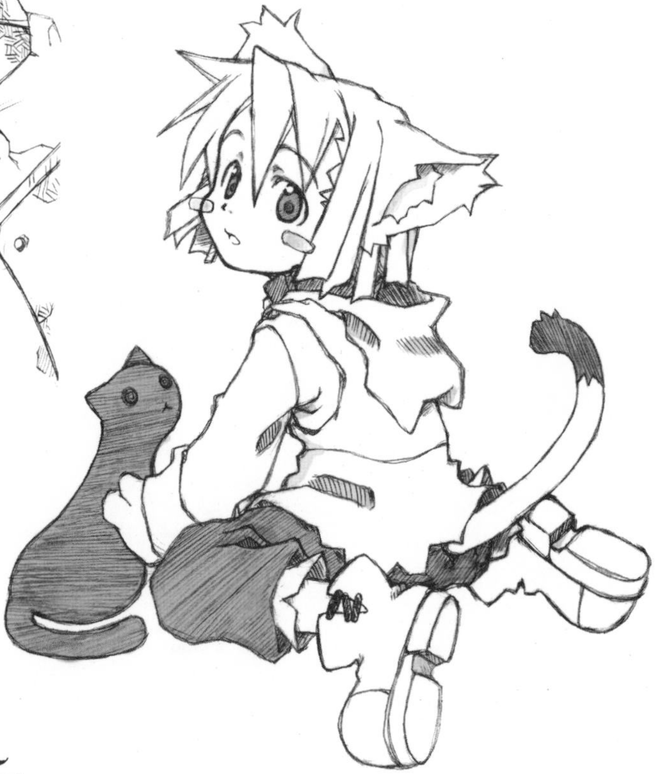

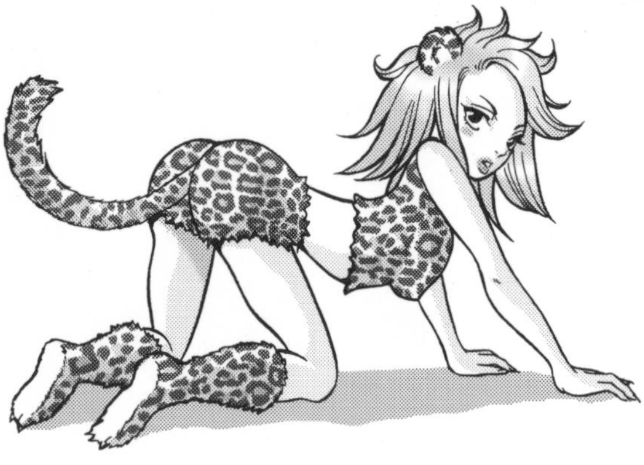

Add a cat's tail and some ears. These characters look very appropriate for a mysterious story.

Chapter 2

Drawing the Face, Hands and Legs

The face is the most important part of any character. Drawing different kinds of faces with various expressions, (a friendly face, an evil face, or a face crying and laughing at the same time) require advanced skills. Understanding the basic structure of the head and how to use patterns and exaggeration is the quickest way to improve your technique.

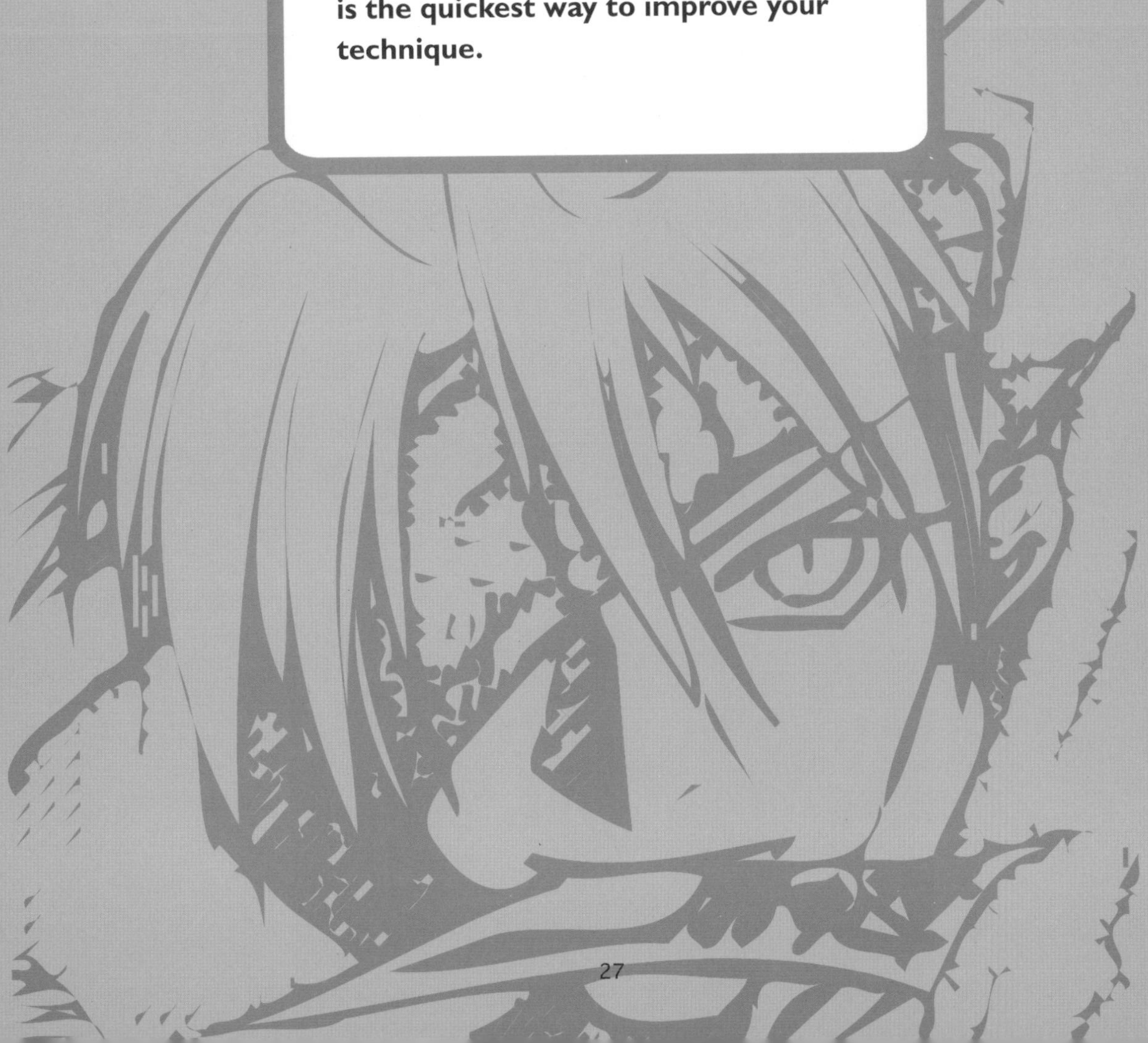

Basics for Drawing the Face 1

The standard way to create a face is to draw an egg-shaped oval and add a cross (+).

Drawing Faces of Male, Female and Children

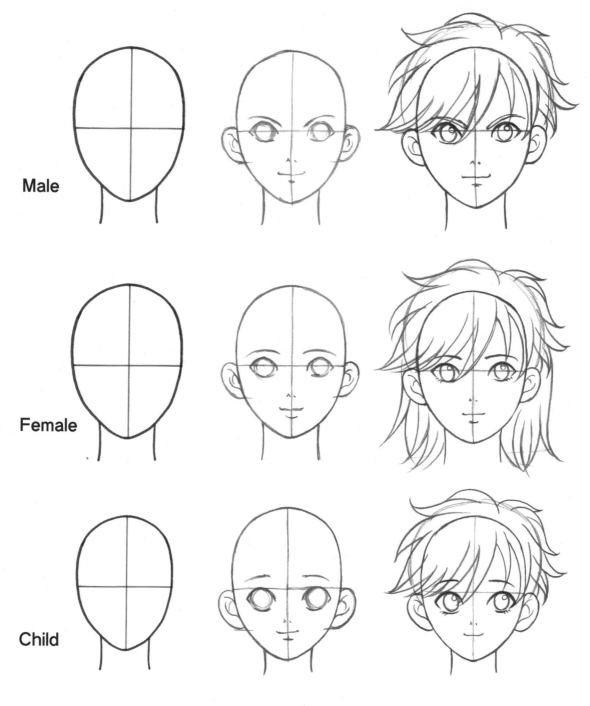

Male

Female

Child

◆The closer the eyes and mouth are, more childish the face looks.

Make rough sketches of egg-shaped ovals and crosses.
Use the lines of the cross to place the eyes, nose and mouth.

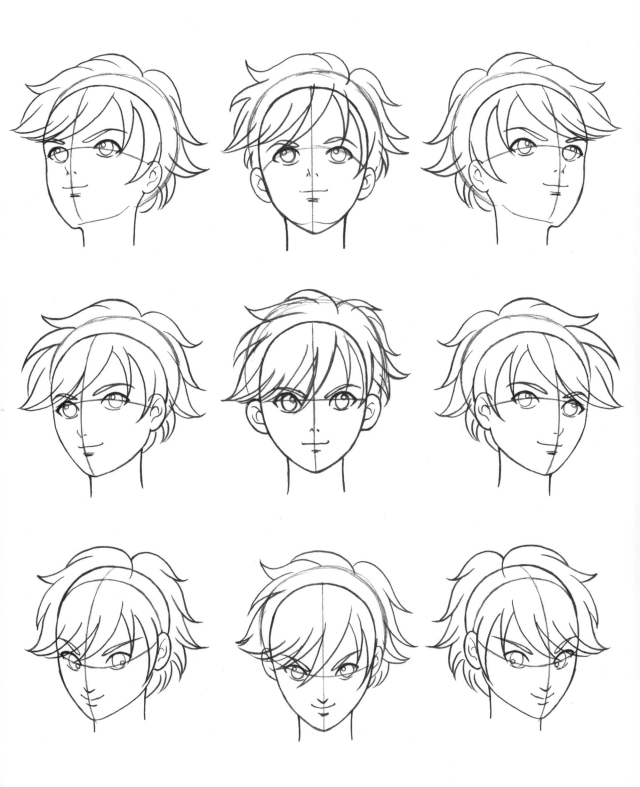

Using Patterns - The Face

The fundamental structure of the face is that the eyes and the ears line up on the same line. The space between the eyes should be about the size of an eye. The forehead, the space between the eyebrows and the bottom of the nose, and the space between the bottom of the nose to the chin should all be the same, also.

Basic Structure of the Face

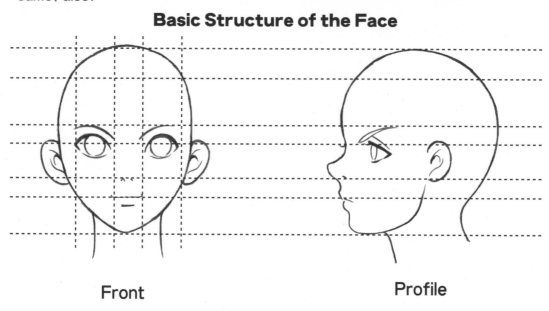

Front Profile

Front

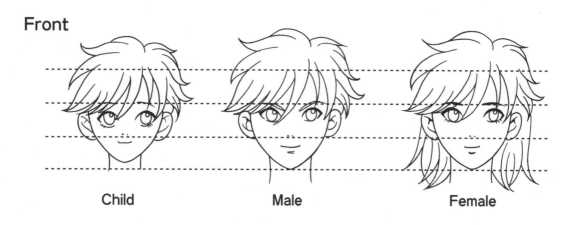

Child Male Female

Profile

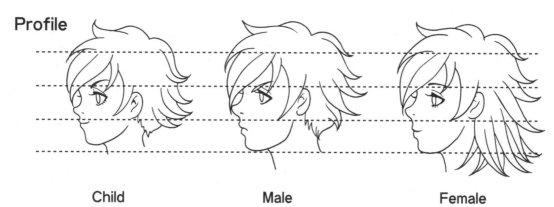

Child Male Female

The Difference Between Realistic Full-figure, Fine-line Sketch, and Simplified Anime Style Faces

Realistic Full-figure Style

Fine-line Sketch Style

Simplified Anime Style

Basics for Drawing the Face 2

Characteristics of Different Facial Shapes

※The hair-style, eyes, noses, and mouths remain the same.

Different Shapes   Male   Female

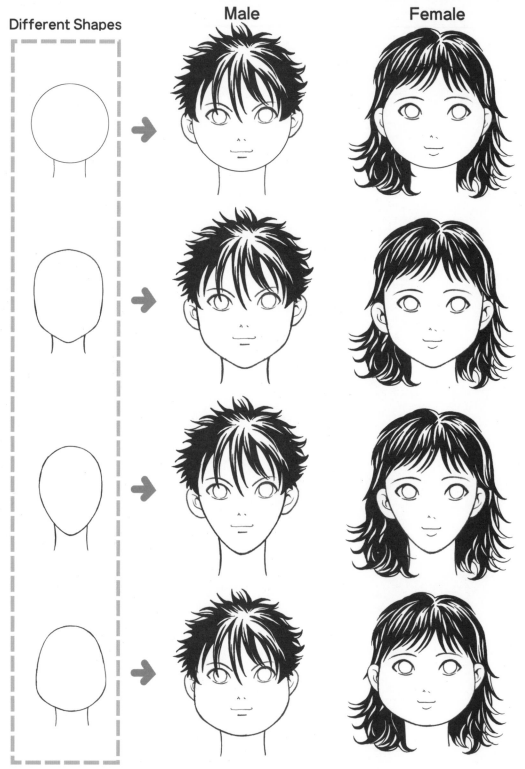

Changing the Shapes of Eyes, Nose, Mouth and Hair

※The hair style and the shape of the face remain the same.

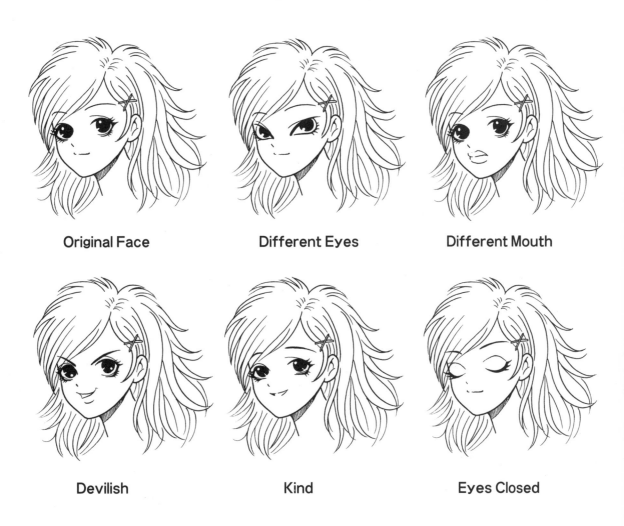

Original Face

Different Eyes

Different Mouth

Devilish

Kind

Eyes Closed

●Variation on the Original Face

As a Boy

Adding Glasses

Different Hair - style

Exaggeration of Facial Shapes

●Different Positions of Nose and Mouth of Each Style

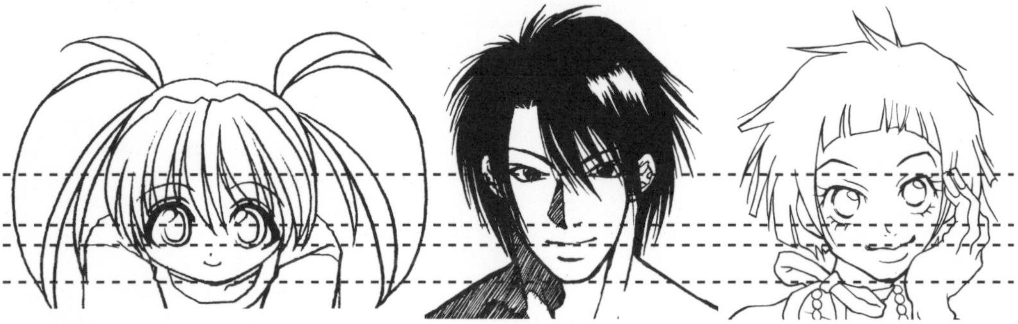

Simplified Anime Style   Realistic Full-figure Style   Fine-line Sketch Style

●Important Points

□Childish and Round
The whole face is exaggerated. Reduced chin, enlarged eyes and very small mouth. Nose is reduced to a dot.

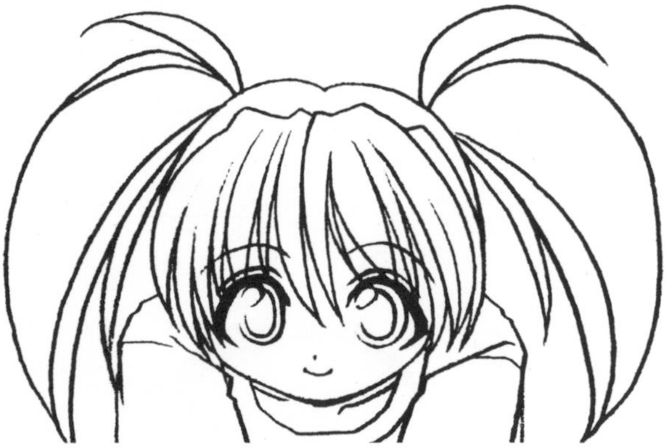

□Egg-Shaped and Narrow
This style is realistic with the sizes of the eyes and mouth, and the length of the nose close to the real human face.

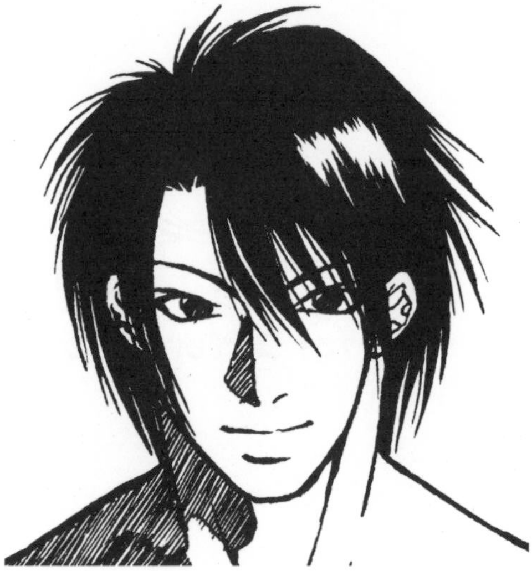

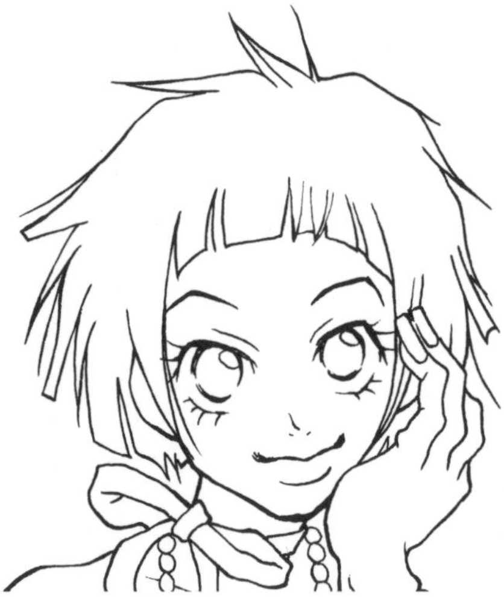

□Sharp and Pointy Chin
Although the shape of the face is very close to human's, the eyes are greatly exaggerated and the nose is reduced to a point. The mouth is enlarged.

Drawing the Eyes
Try to find your style

Realistic Eyes and *Manga* Eyes

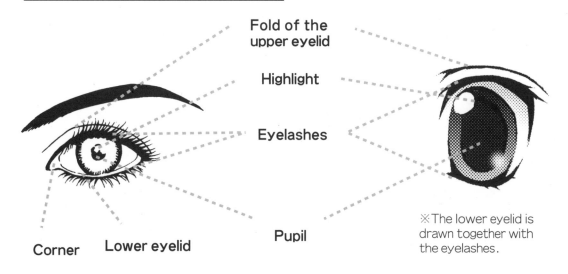

- Fold of the upper eyelid
- Highlight
- Eyelashes
- Pupil
- Corner
- Lower eyelid

※The lower eyelid is drawn together with the eyelashes.

Male and Female Eyes

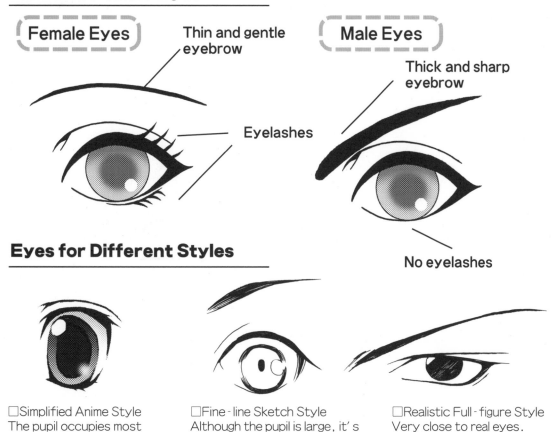

Female Eyes
- Thin and gentle eyebrow
- Eyelashes

Male Eyes
- Thick and sharp eyebrow
- No eyelashes

Eyes for Different Styles

□Simplified Anime Style
The pupil occupies most of the eye leaving little space for the white part.

□Fine - line Sketch Style
Although the pupil is large, it's not large as much as the Anime Style eyes. The white portion only takes up small space.

□Realistic Full - figure Style
Very close to real eyes. Understated highlights.

Exaggeration of the Eyes and Using Models

Normal   Angry   Surprised   Laughing

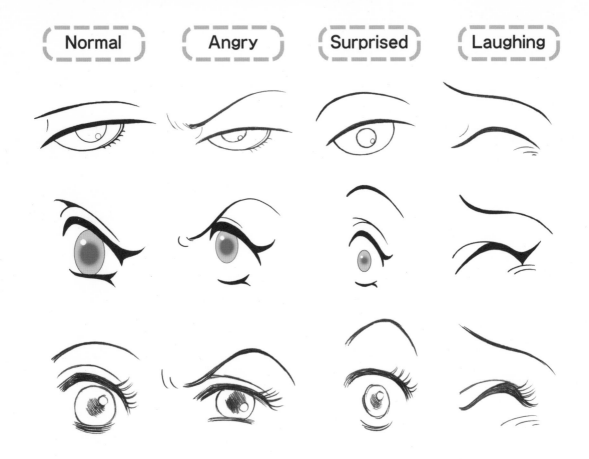

Impression of Different Eyes

The hair-style, the shape of the face, nose, and mouth remain the same.

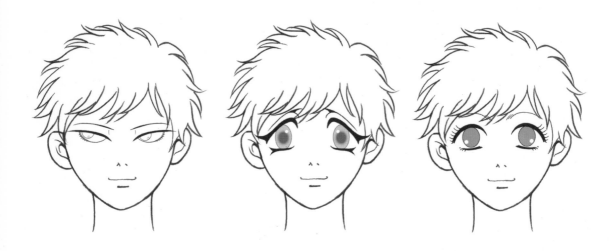

Drawing the Nose and Mouth

Realistic Nose and *Manga* Nose

Realistic

Manga

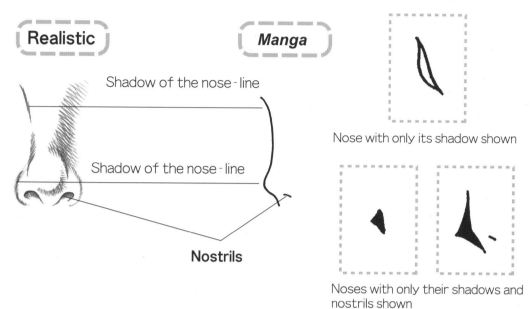

Shadow of the nose - line

Shadow of the nose - line

Nostrils

Simplified Manga Nose

Nose with only its shadow shown

Noses with only their shadows and nostrils shown

Realistic Mouth and *Manga* Mouth

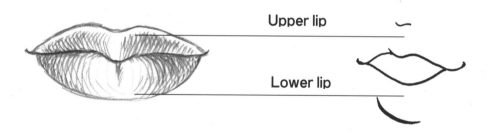

Upper lip

Lower lip

More Simplified *Manga* Mouths

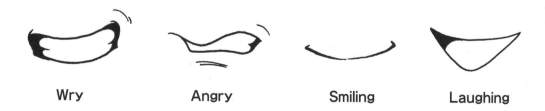

Wry   Angry   Smiling   Laughing

Representation Samples for the Eyes

A: Realistic Full-figure Style

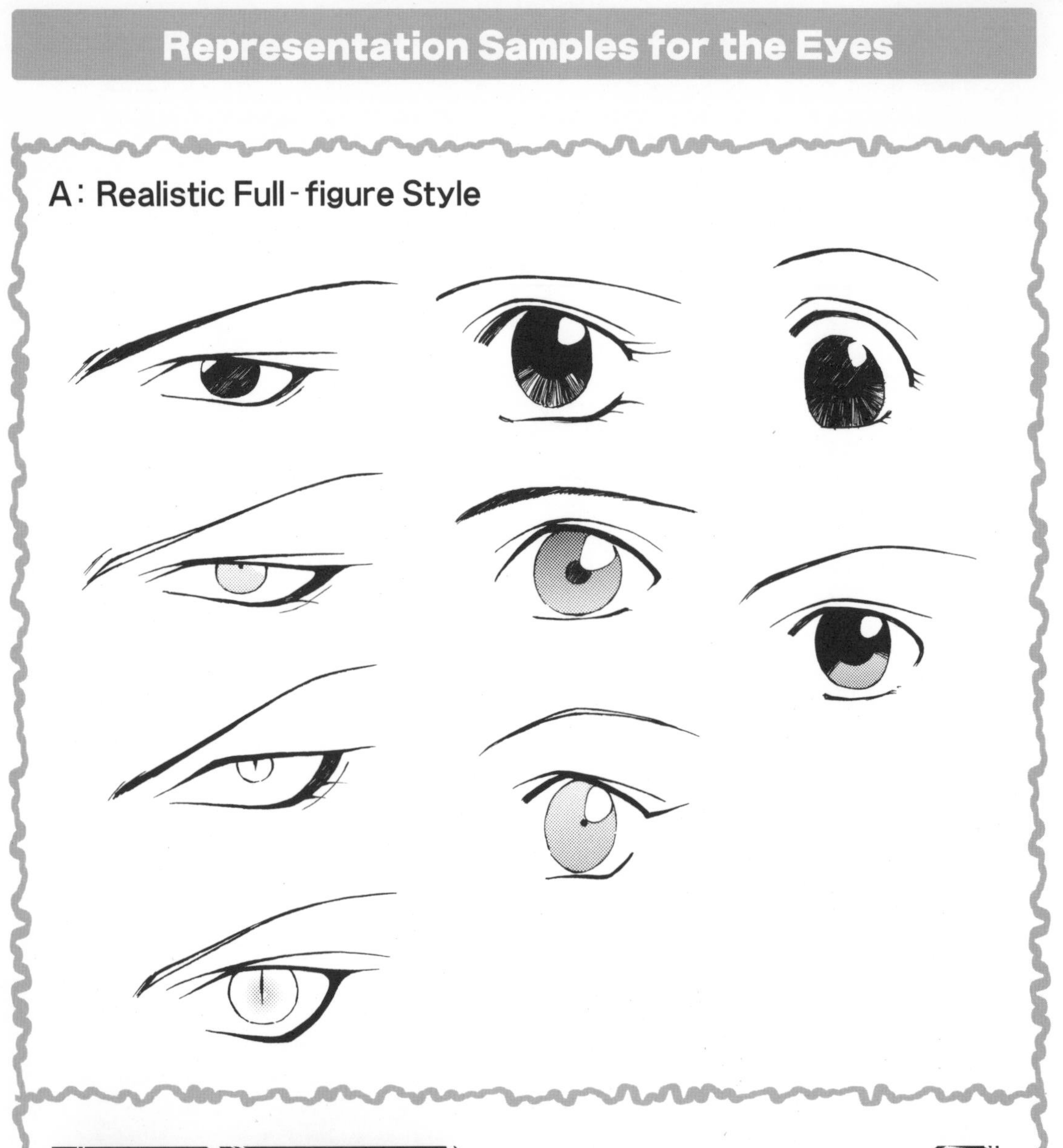

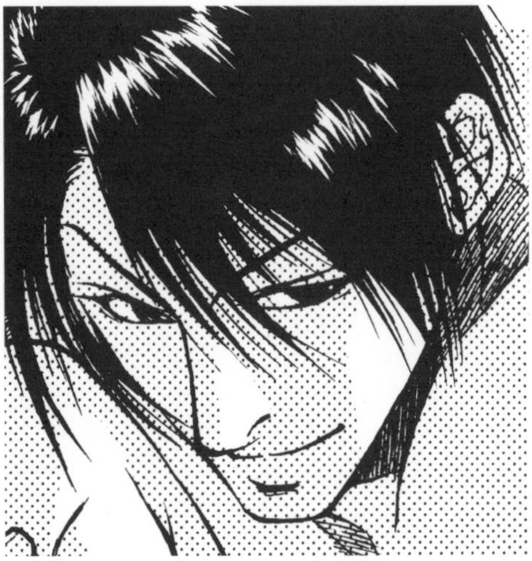

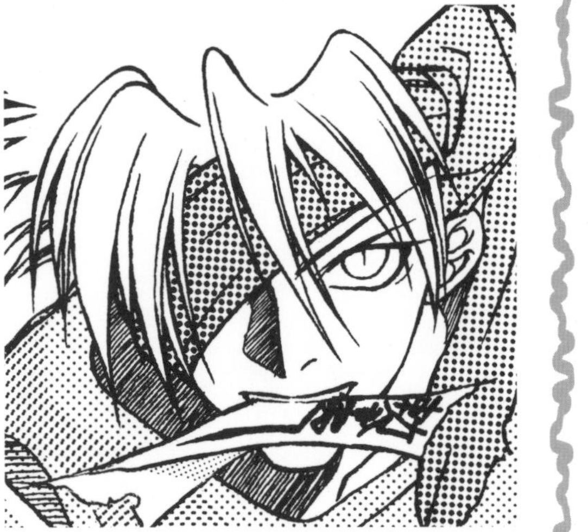

B: Fine-line Sketch Style

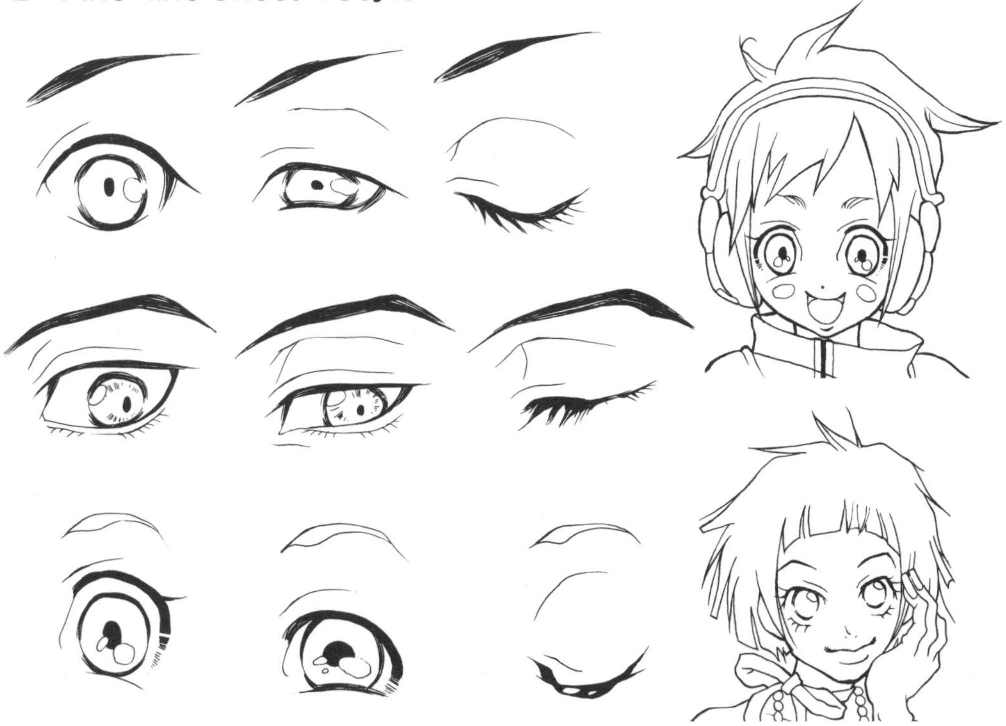

C: Simplified Anime Style

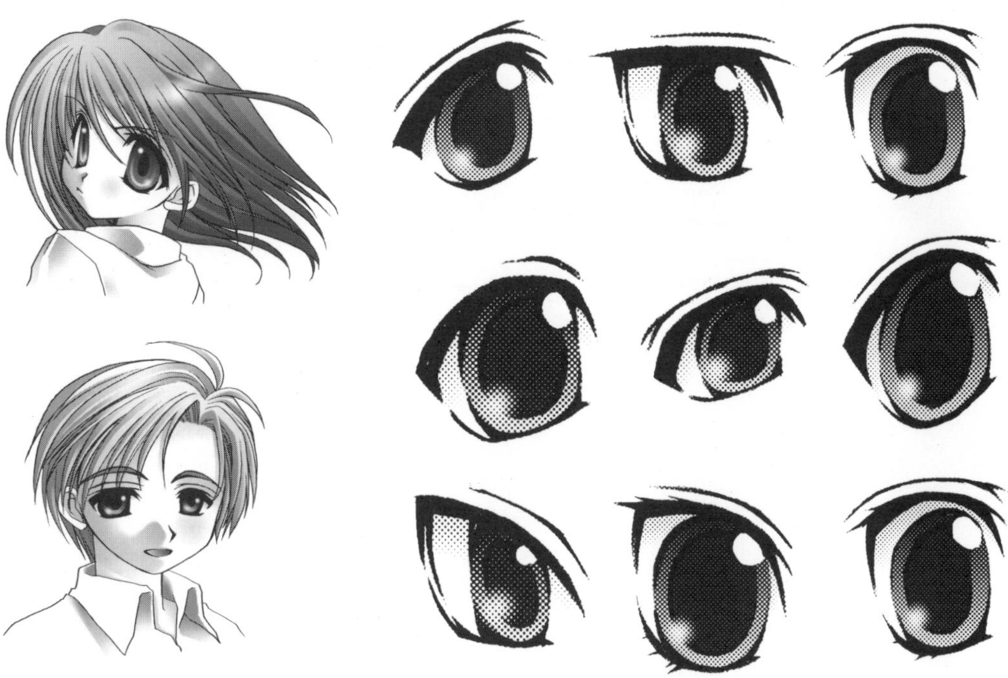

Alternating Facial Expressions

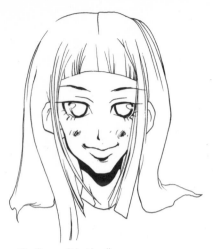

Smiling with the lips

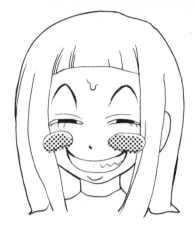

Laughing, with the eyebrows and mouth shaped like crescent

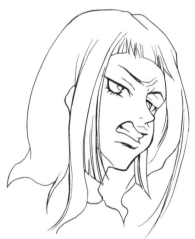

Angry, with eyebrows close together and mouth twisted

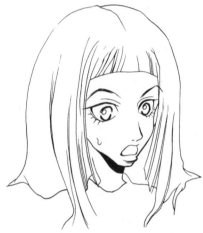

Surprised, with widely opened eyes and mouth

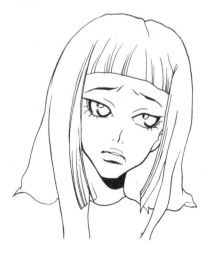

Sad, with lowered lips and tilting neck

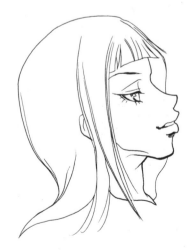

Snobbery, with lifted chin and narrow eyes

Samples of Facial Angles and Expressions Using the Eyes

Upward and downward angles and the position of the eyes can amplify the character' s personality.

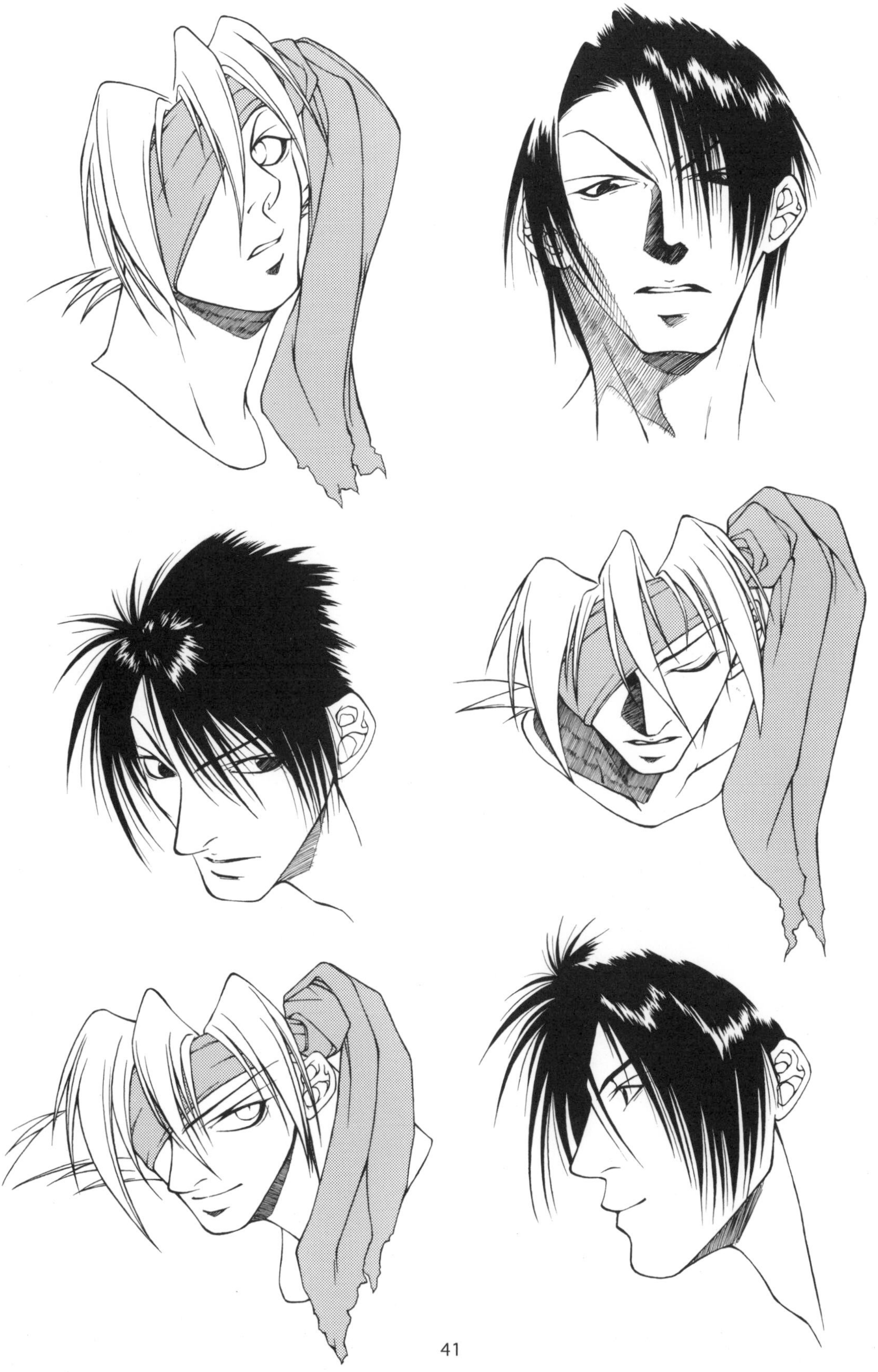

Drawing the Hair

Arranging the Hair.
The hair should be drawn
much larger than the skull.

●Important Points●

The face would
look cuter if you
arrange the hair
much larger than
the face.

Samples of Different Hair · Styles

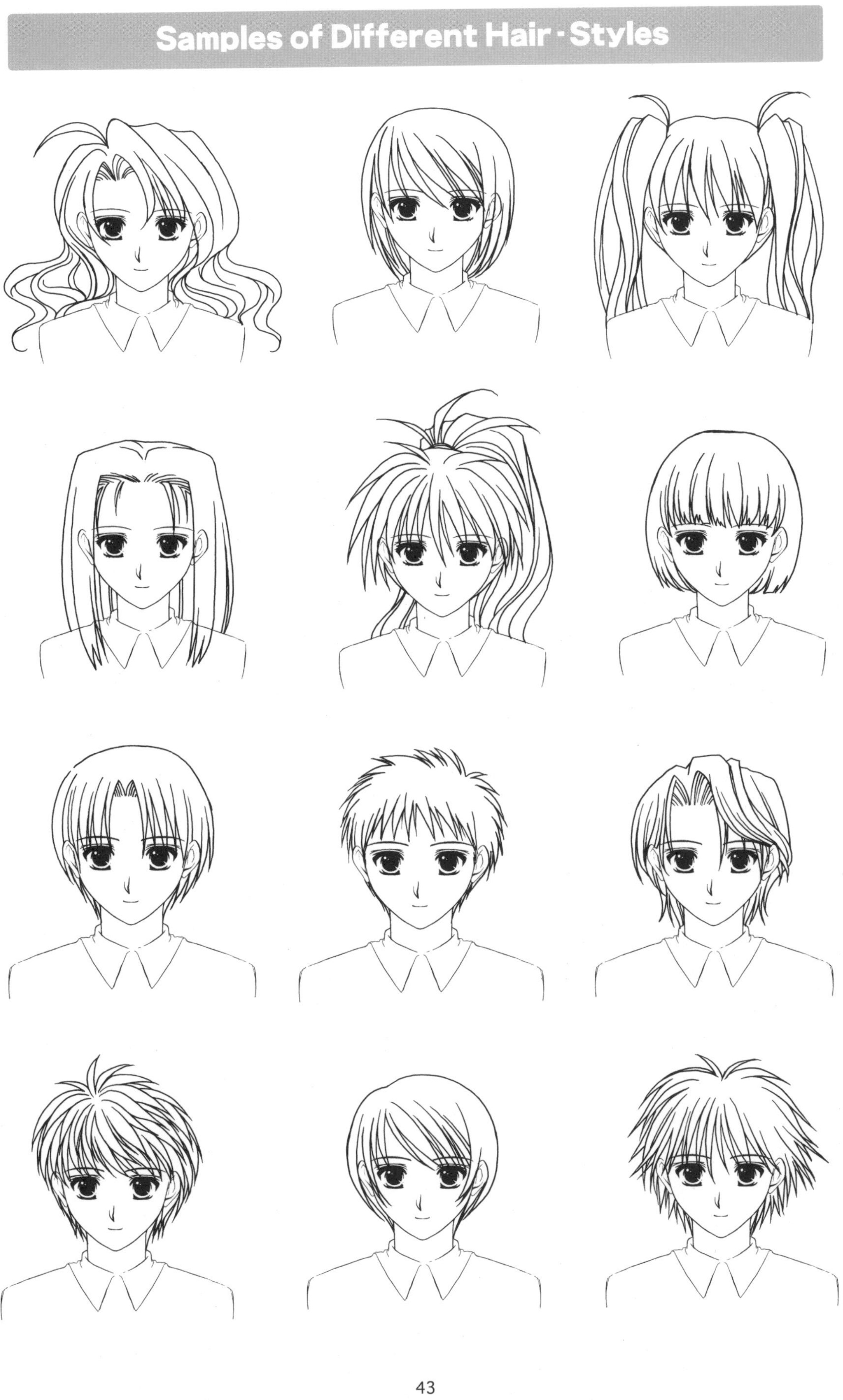

Drawing the Hands

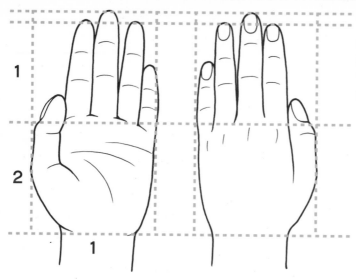

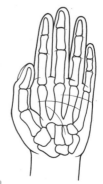

The length of the index finger and the ring finger should be about the same. The middle finger should be as long as the palm and the back of the hand.

●The Difference Between Male and Female Hands●

Female hands are thin, small and smooth. On the other hand, male hands are big and rough with large knuckles. Female hands should have long and manicured nails while male hand should have short and square nails.

●Hand Movements

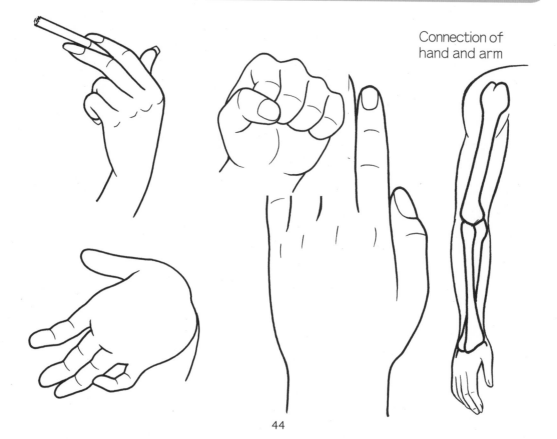

Connection of hand and arm

Samples of Different Hand Pose

●Opened

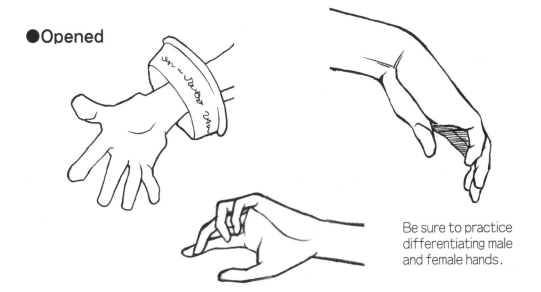

Be sure to practice differentiating male and female hands.

●Closed

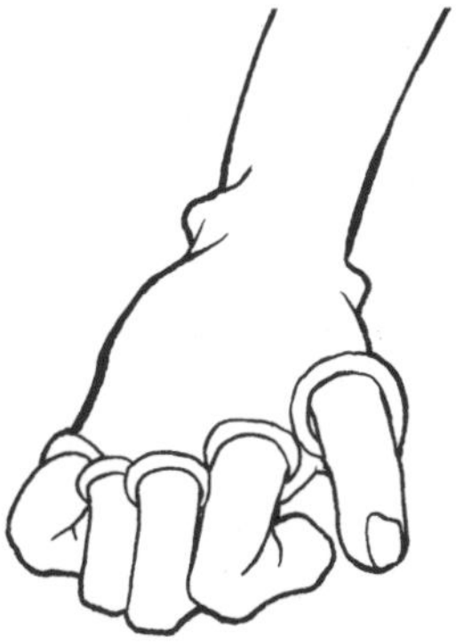

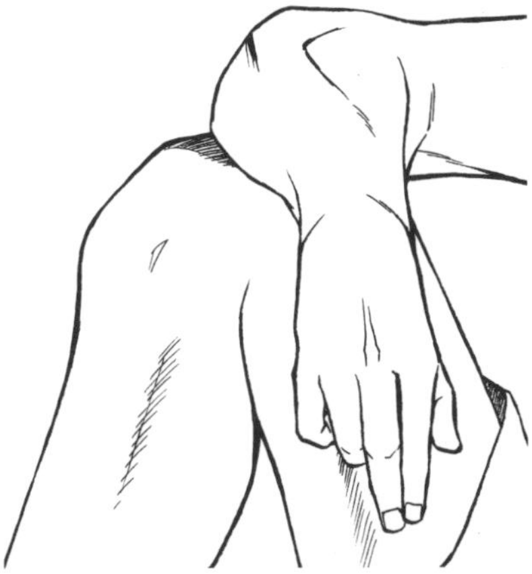

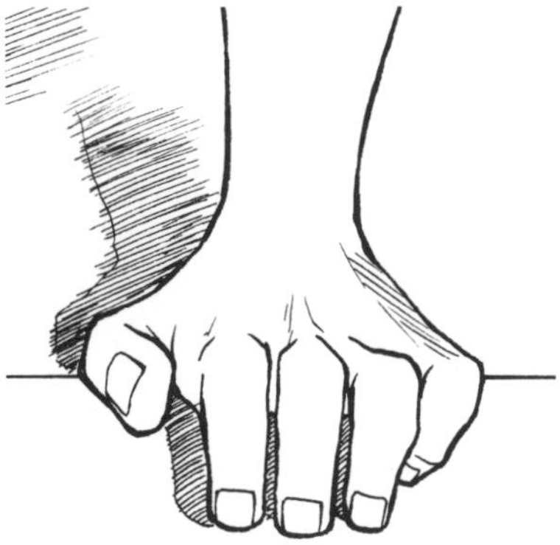

45

●Arranging the Toes

Bare feet should be arranged so that the each foot is facing the opposite sides and would make a triangle. Female feet should be drawn closer together.

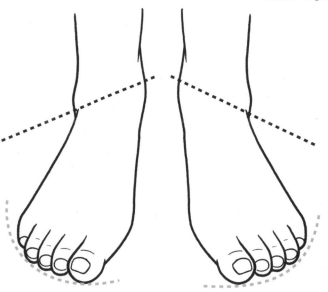

●Feet with Heels

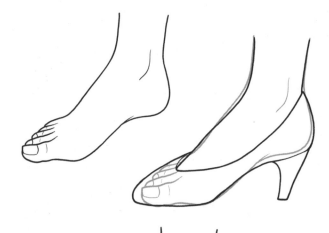

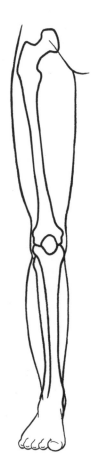

Connection of leg and foot

Samples of Different Foot Pose

●Bare

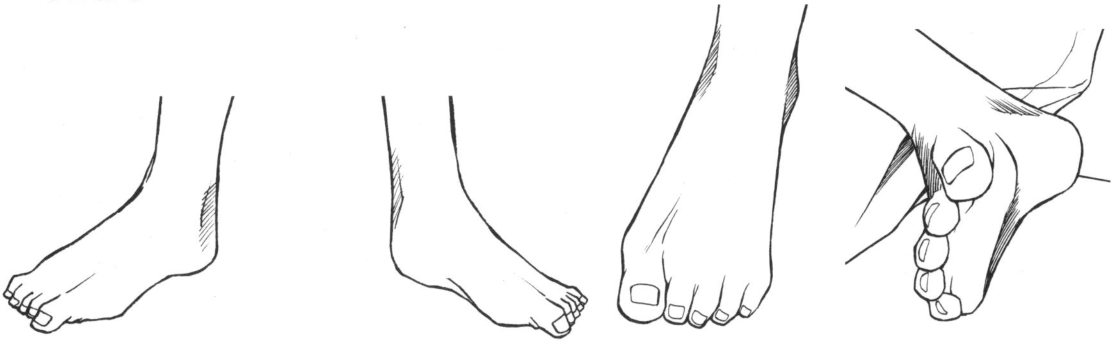

●With Sandals and Boots

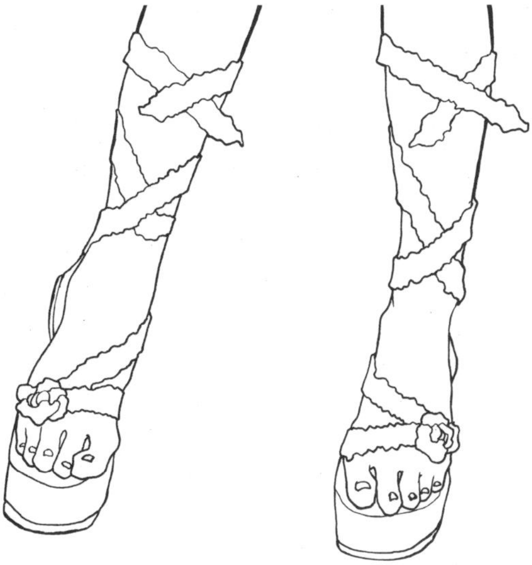

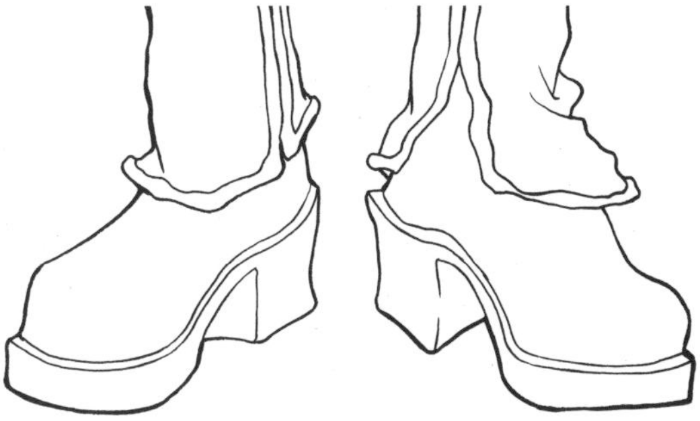

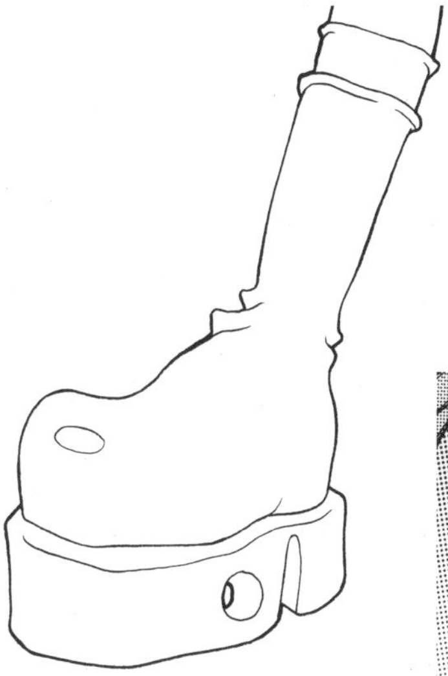

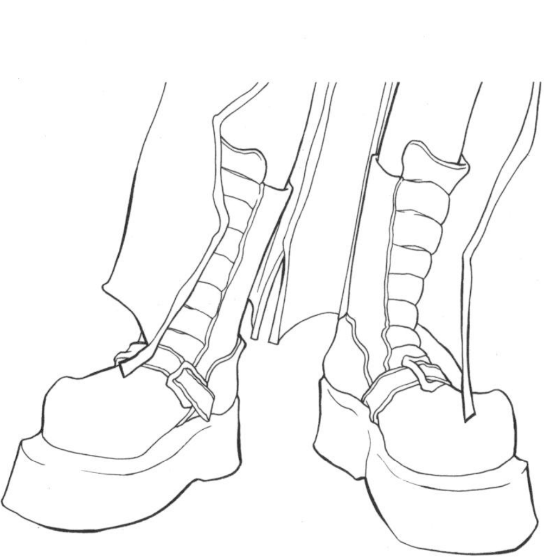

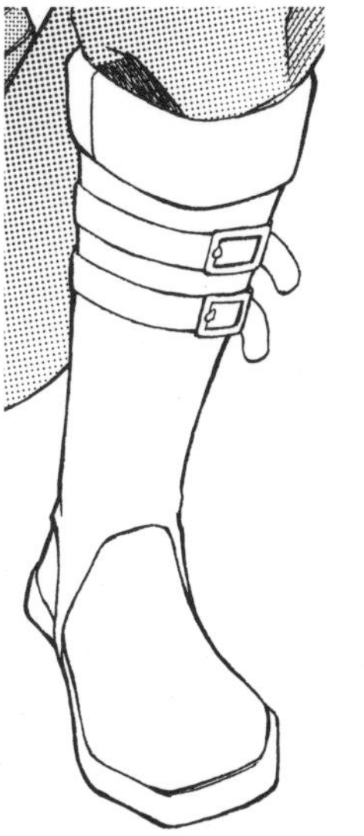

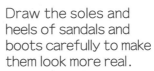

Draw the soles and heels of sandals and boots carefully to make them look more real.

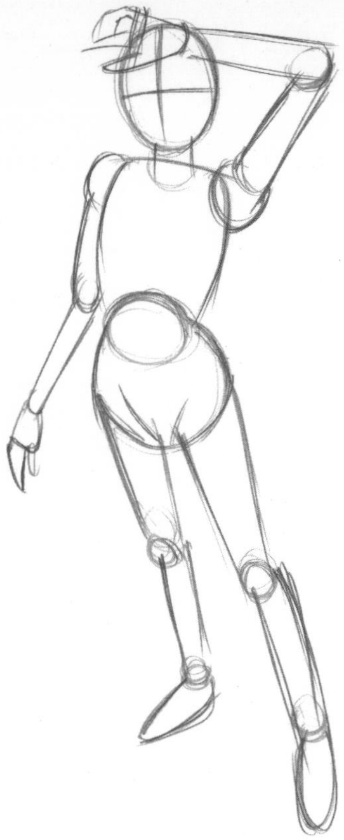

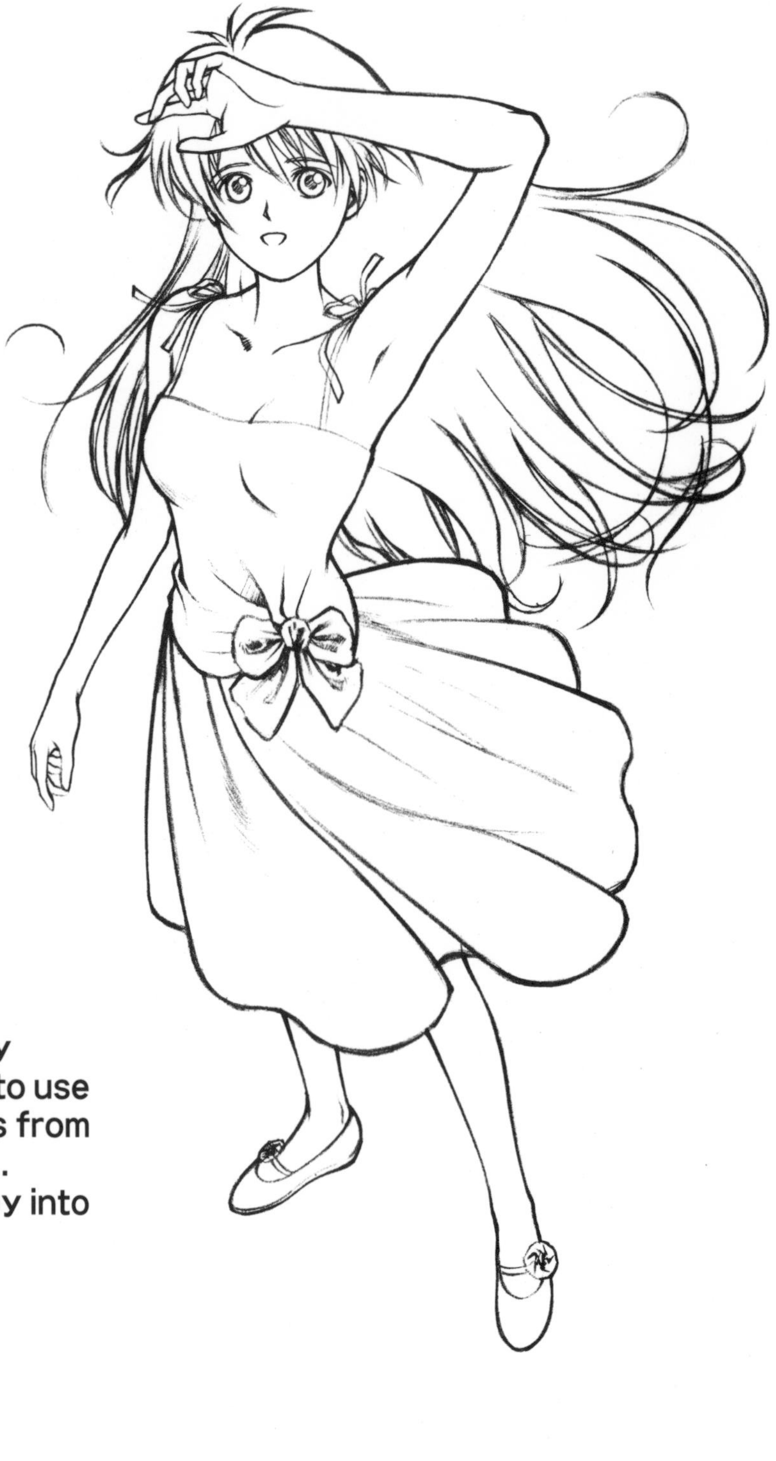

In order to create lively characters, you need to use vivid and dynamic lines from the sketching process.
Try to add some energy into them.

Chapter 3

Drawing the Whole Body

Now that you know the basics of creating characters, let's proceed by looking at some characters created using the three different styles. Learn how to draw with the style you like.

A: Drawing Realistic Full-figure Style Characters

B: Drawing Fine-line Sketch Style Characters

C: Drawing Simplified Anime Style Characters

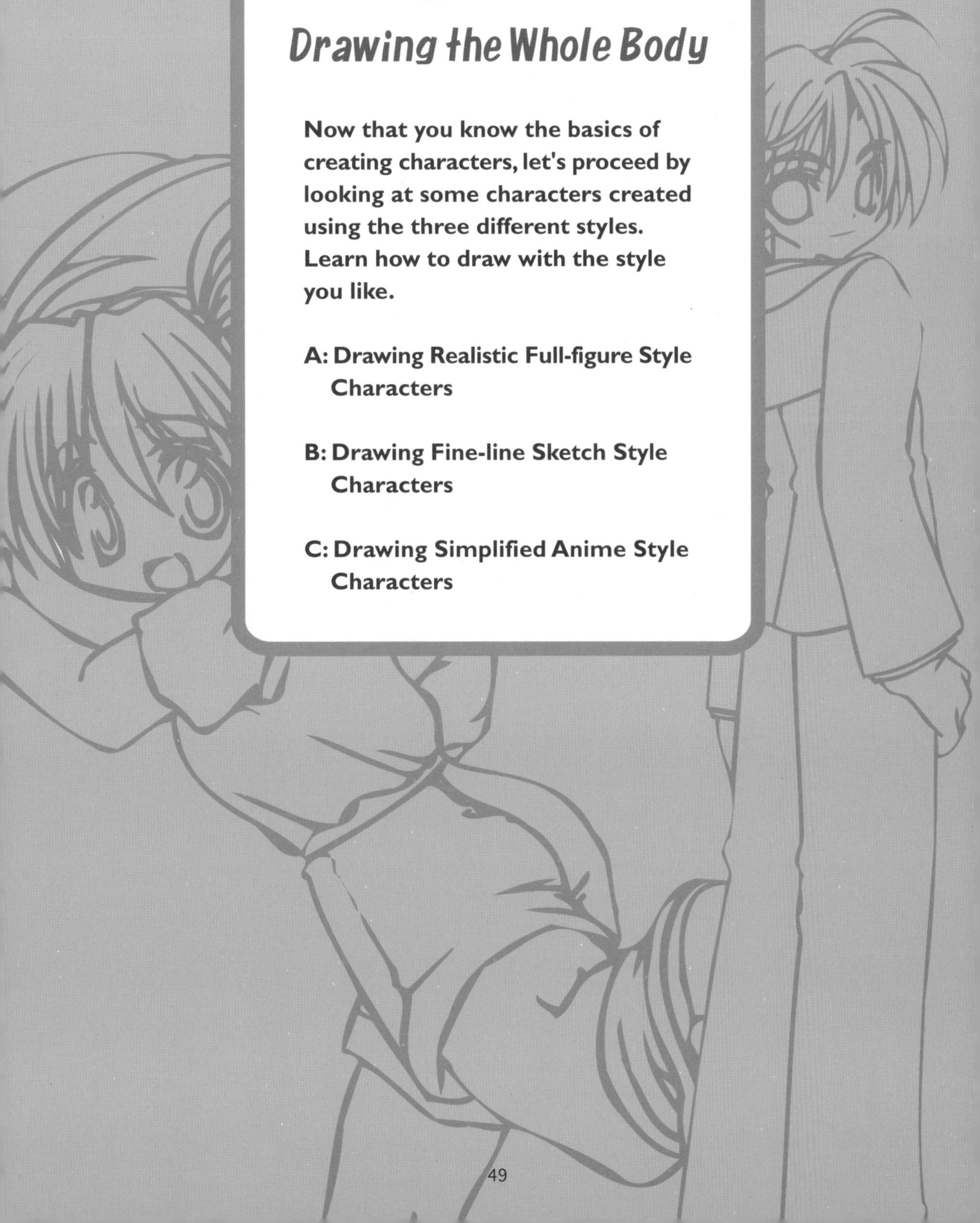

A: Drawing Realistic Full-figure Style Characters

Drawing realistic full-figure style characters involves using accurate sketches of human body as the base.

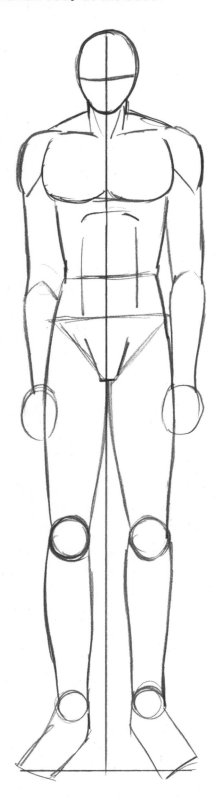

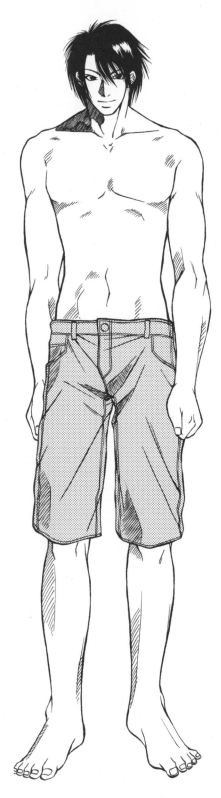

The Drawing Process

① Sketch out the human body with keeping the head - torso balance in mind.

② Add muscle tones and hair.

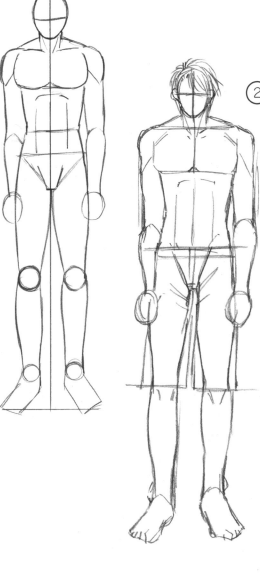

③ Using a pencil, draw out the final outline.

④ Trace the lines with a pen and finish.

Character Chart

Be sure to draw out the front, side and back of the main characters beforehand.

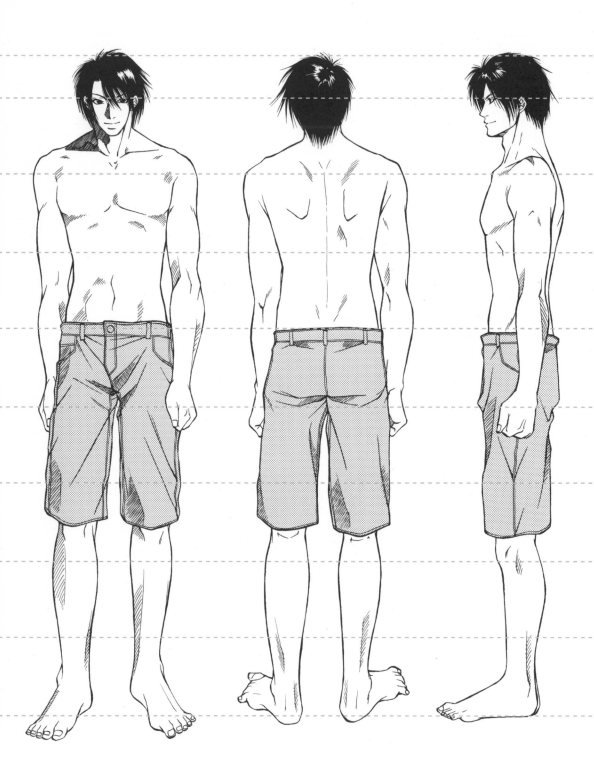

Creating Two Characters by Changing Head-Torso Scale

By changing their heights, you can easily differentiate a male and a boy character.

Young male' s legs should be longer than the boy' s.
Considering the head as one unit, adult characters usually have 8 head-length bodies

Young Male: 8.5 head-length

Boy: 7 head-length

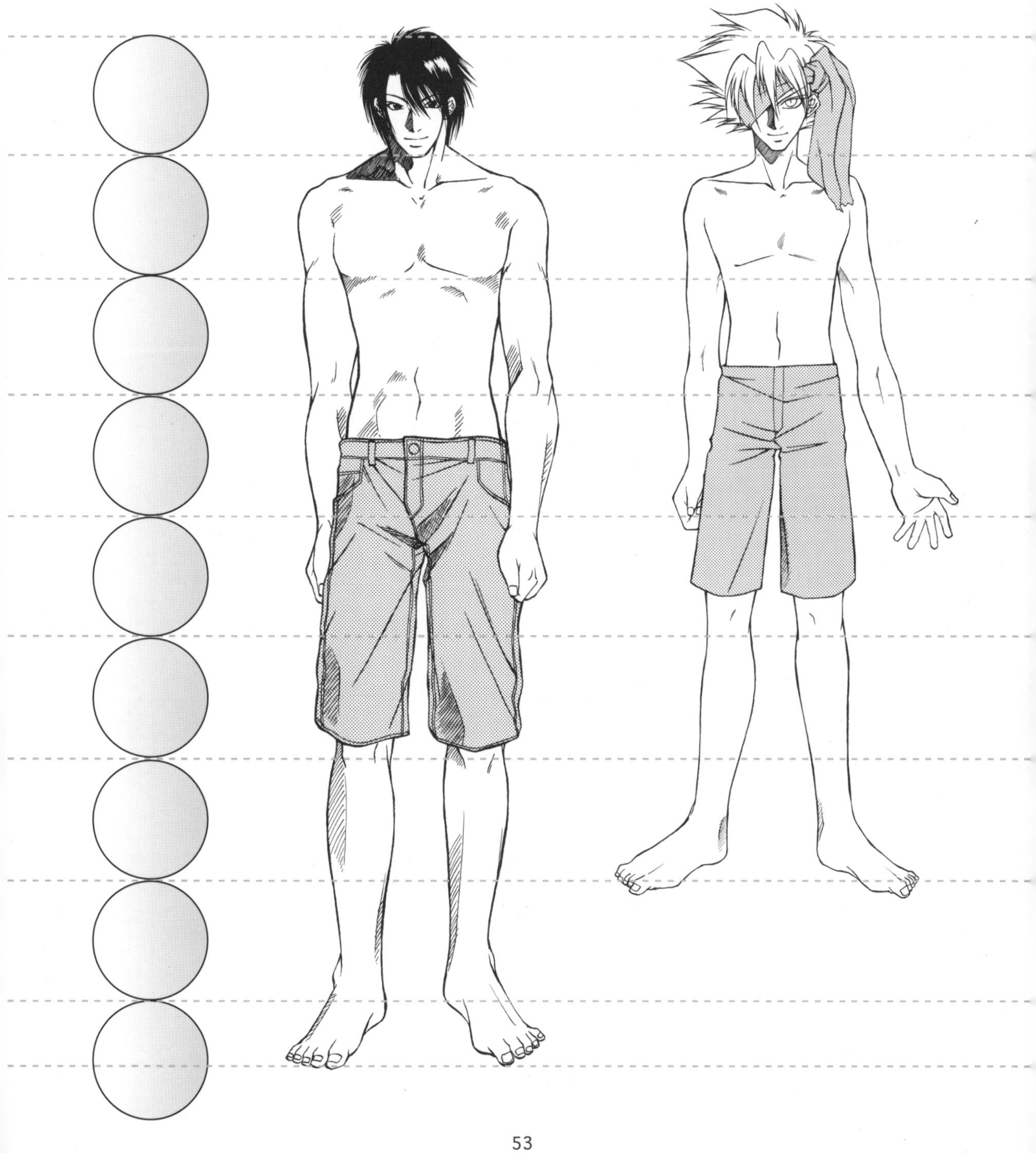

Character Chart -- Young Male and Boy

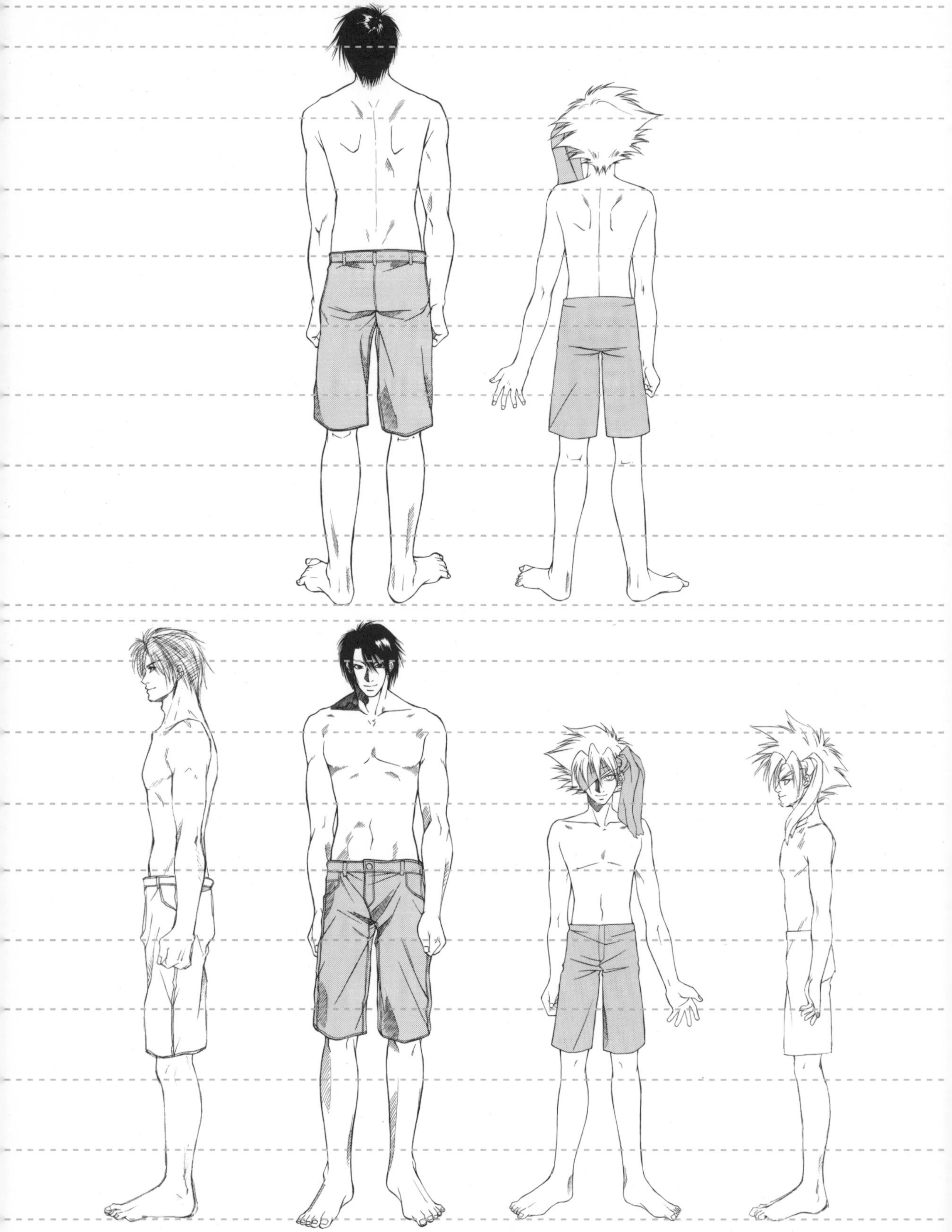

You should also draw them with both upward and downward angles.

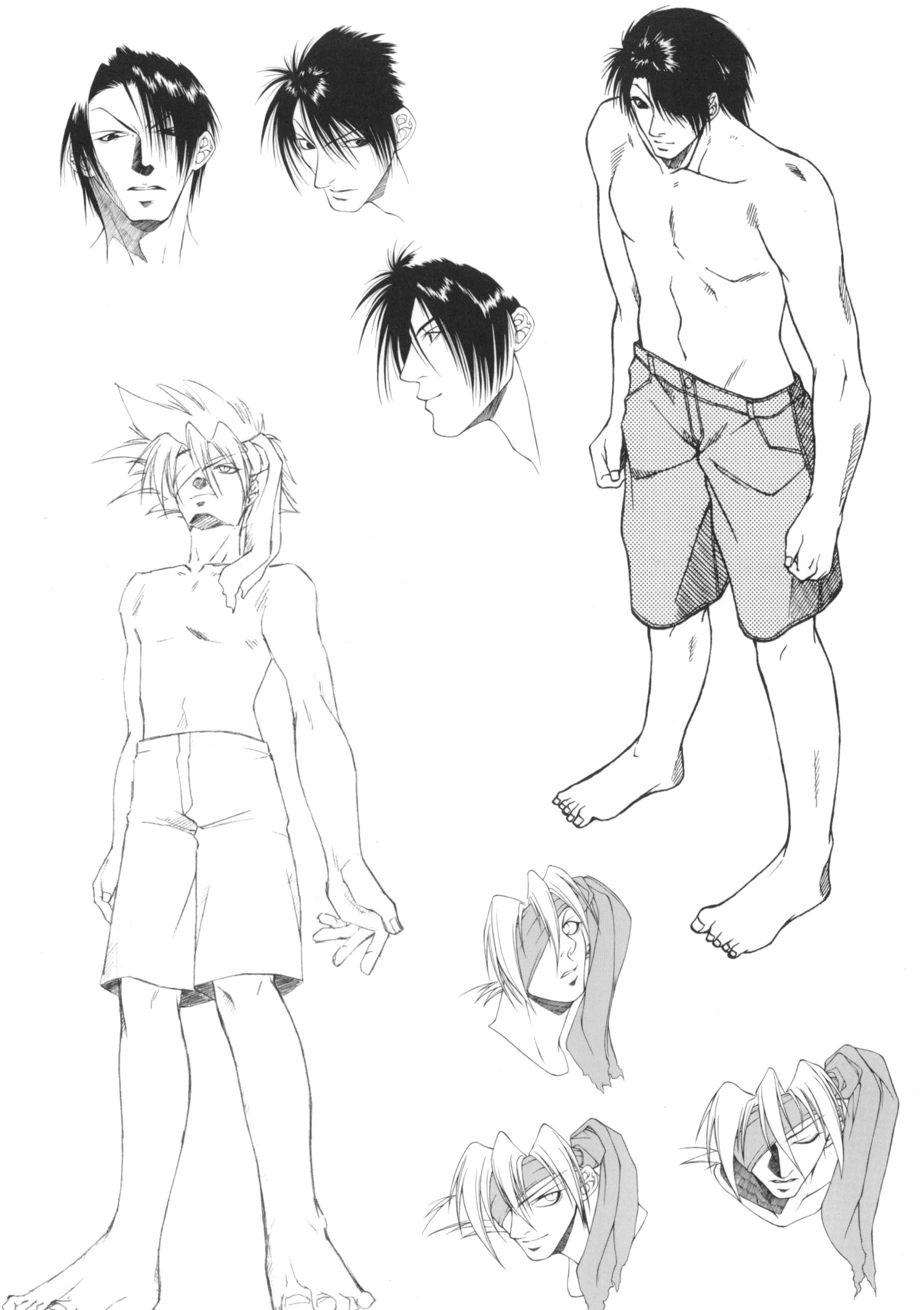

Drawing Characters with Tools/Objects

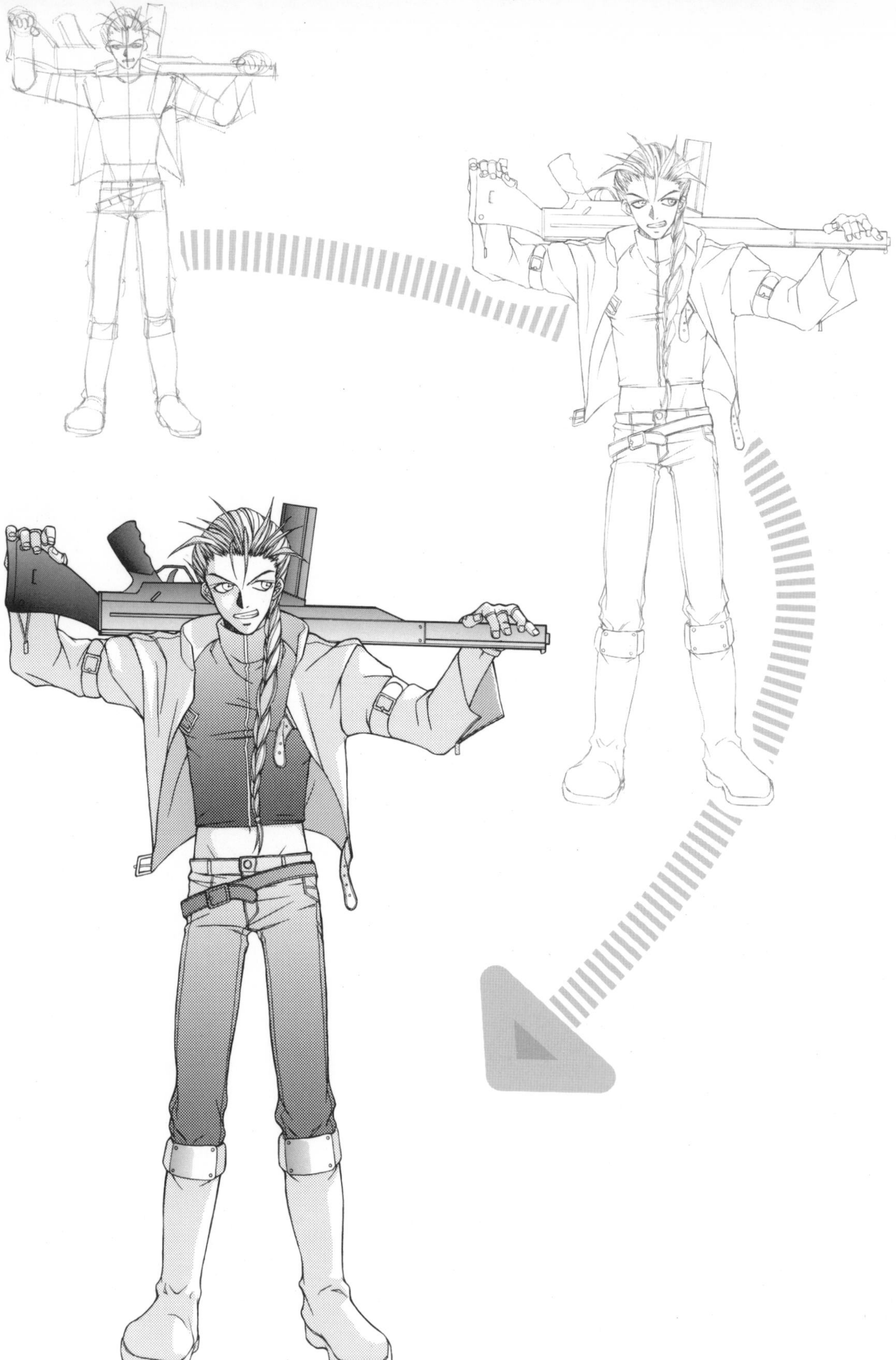

B: Drawing Fine-Line Sketch Style Characters

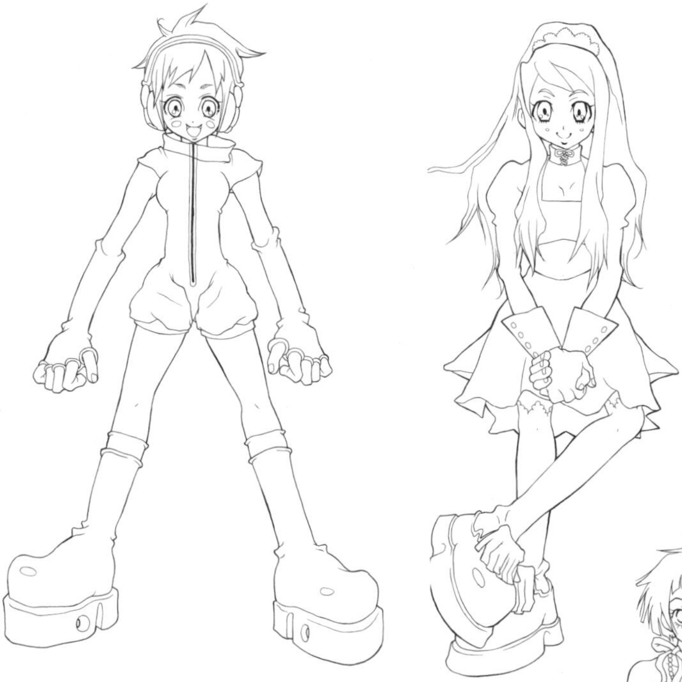

□Game Design Type Characters
Draw using the pattern technique and simplifying them.

□Normal Type Characters
Vivid lines add realistic feeling to them. Dress them fashionably when adding details.

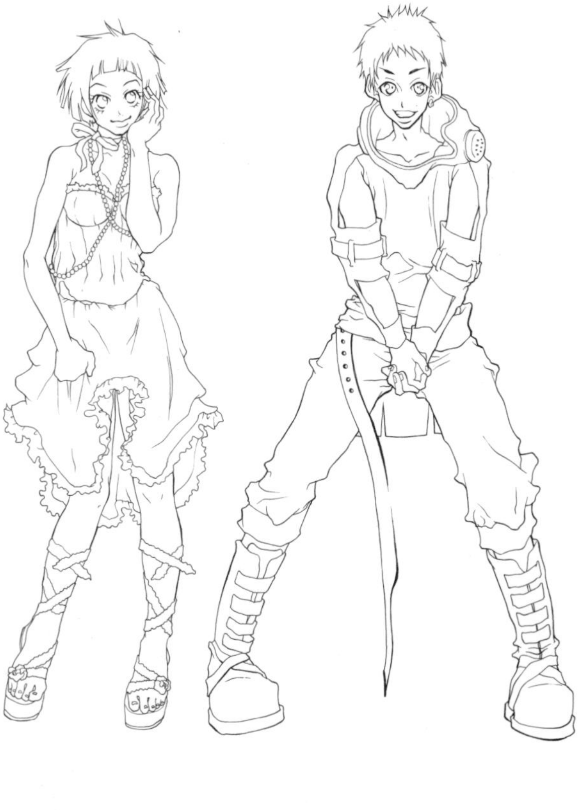

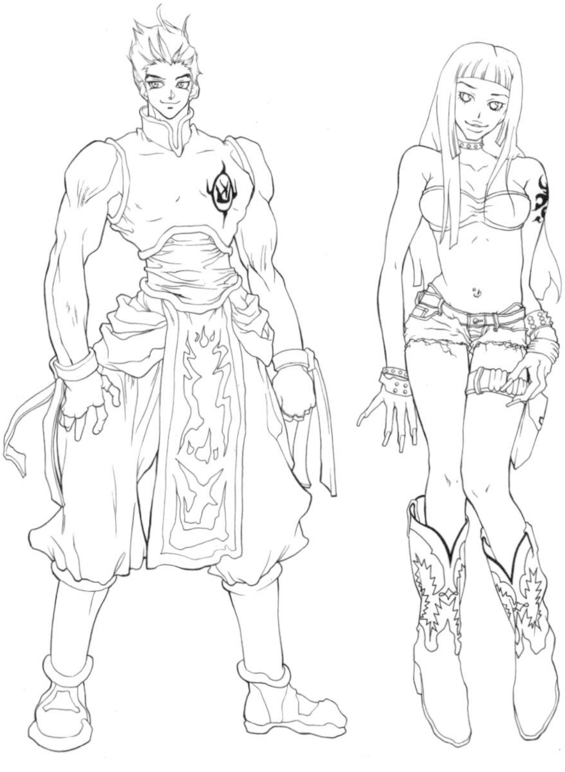

□Fighting Type Characters
Use exaggeration skillfully.

Game Design Type Characters

Decide on a basic shape and sketch out your image.

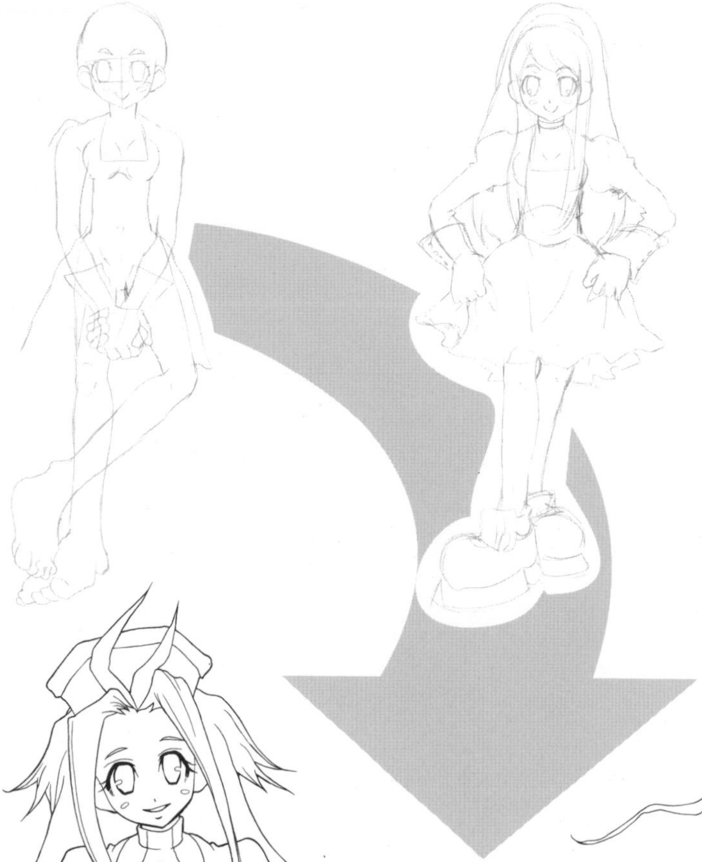

Avoid making them look like anime style characters by leaving out some details to keep the lines light and lively.

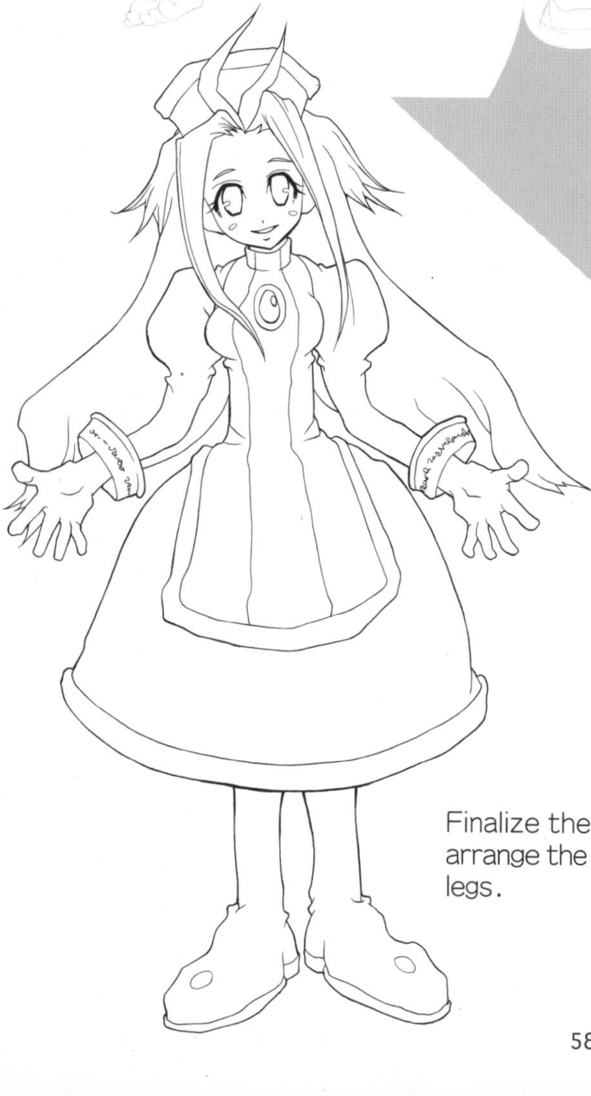

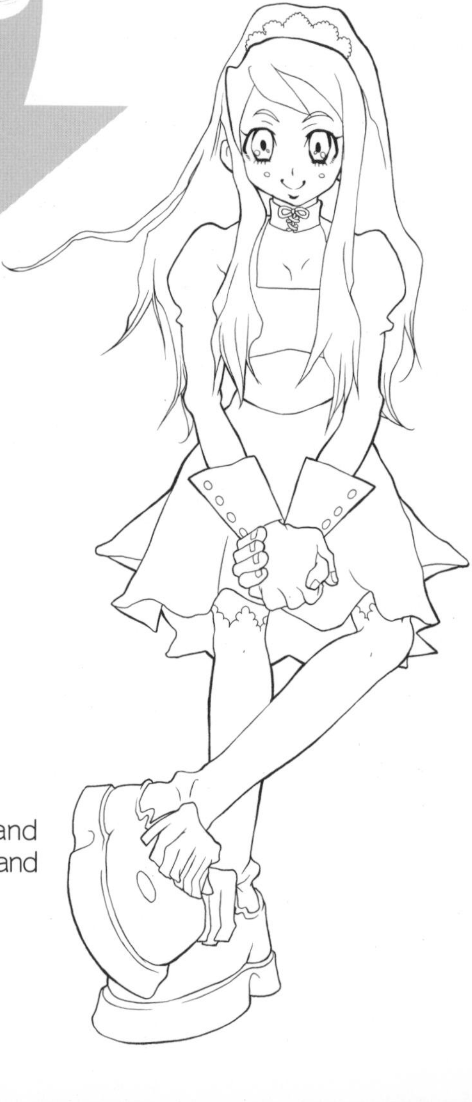

Finalize the pose and arrange the hands and legs.

Normal Type Characters

Add tiny details and fashionable clothes to give originality and personality to the character. The key is the technique to sketch using vivid and lively lines. Comparing to the original sketch, the finished version looks much more alive and attractive. Don' t forget to add details to the face, clothes and hair.

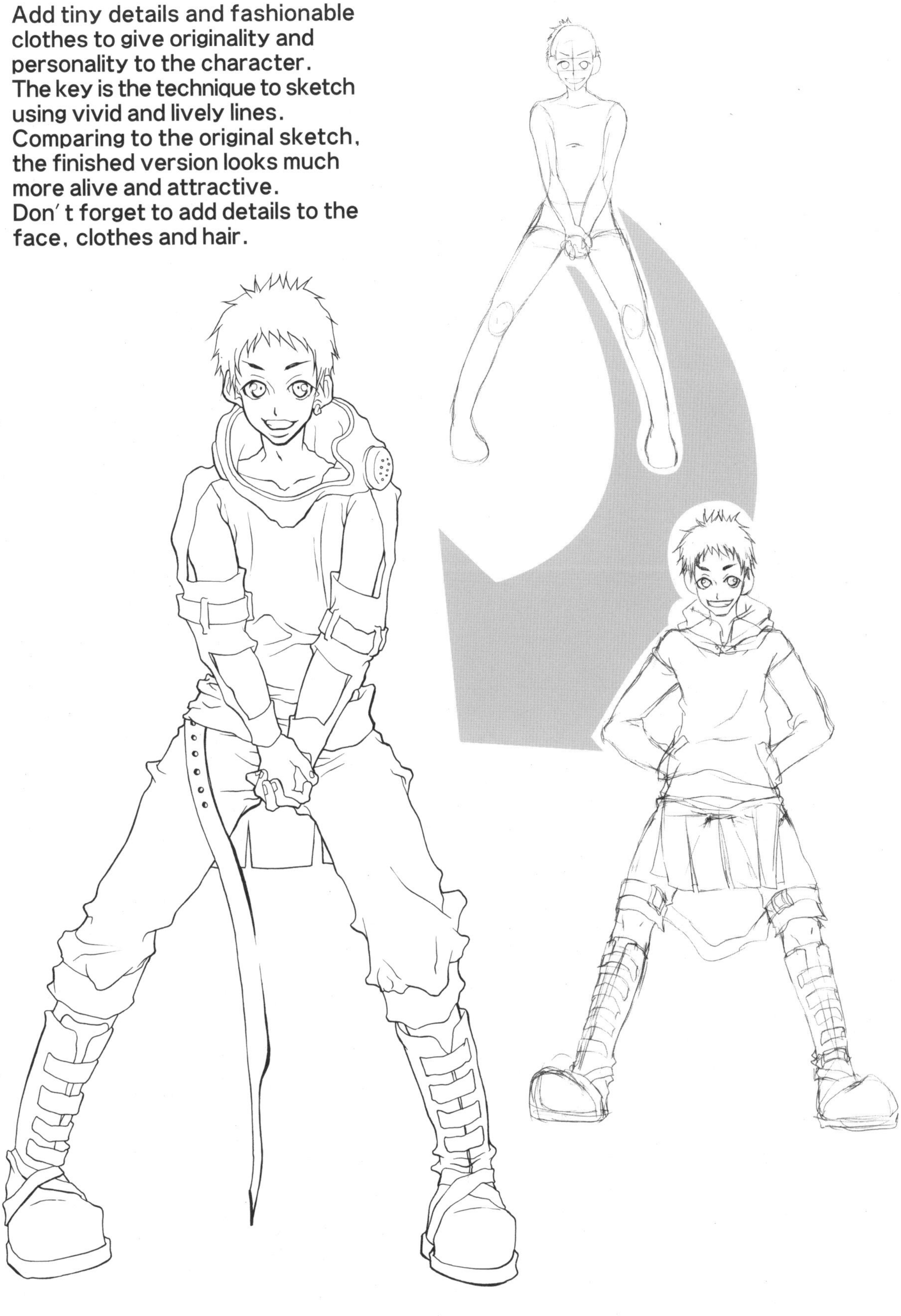

Fighting Type Characters

Use exaggeration to make them look masculine.

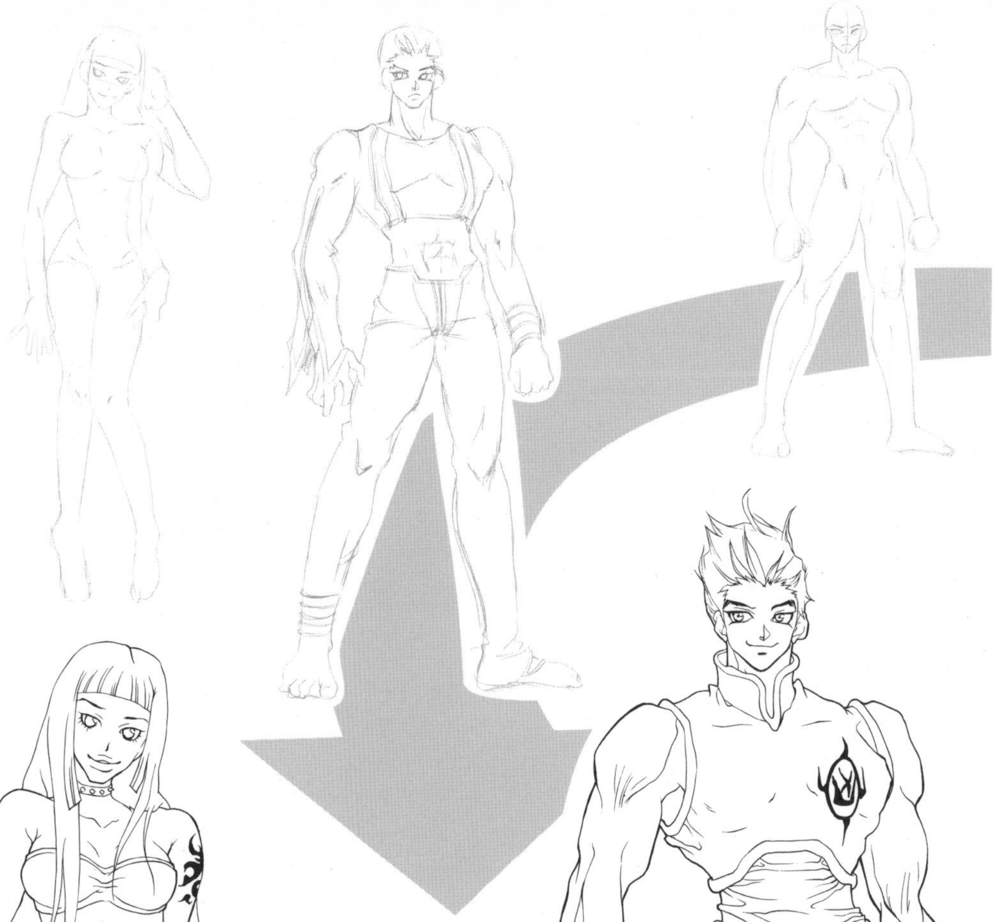

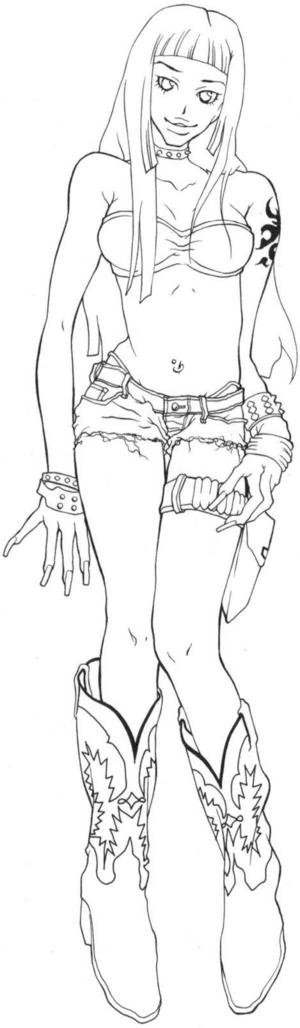

The finished versions are much more exaggerated than the first sketch. Even though the composition and structure become somewhat unbalanced, the characters look more attractive than before.

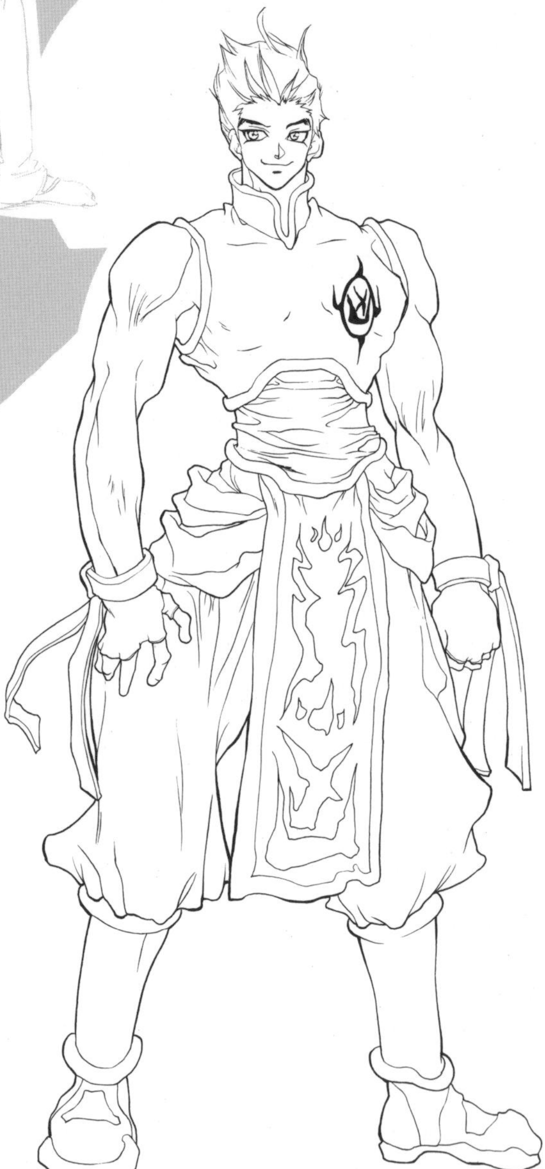

Finished Samples

Exaggeration, elaboration and fashionable clothing on top of the detailed sketches add distinctive atmosphere to these characters.

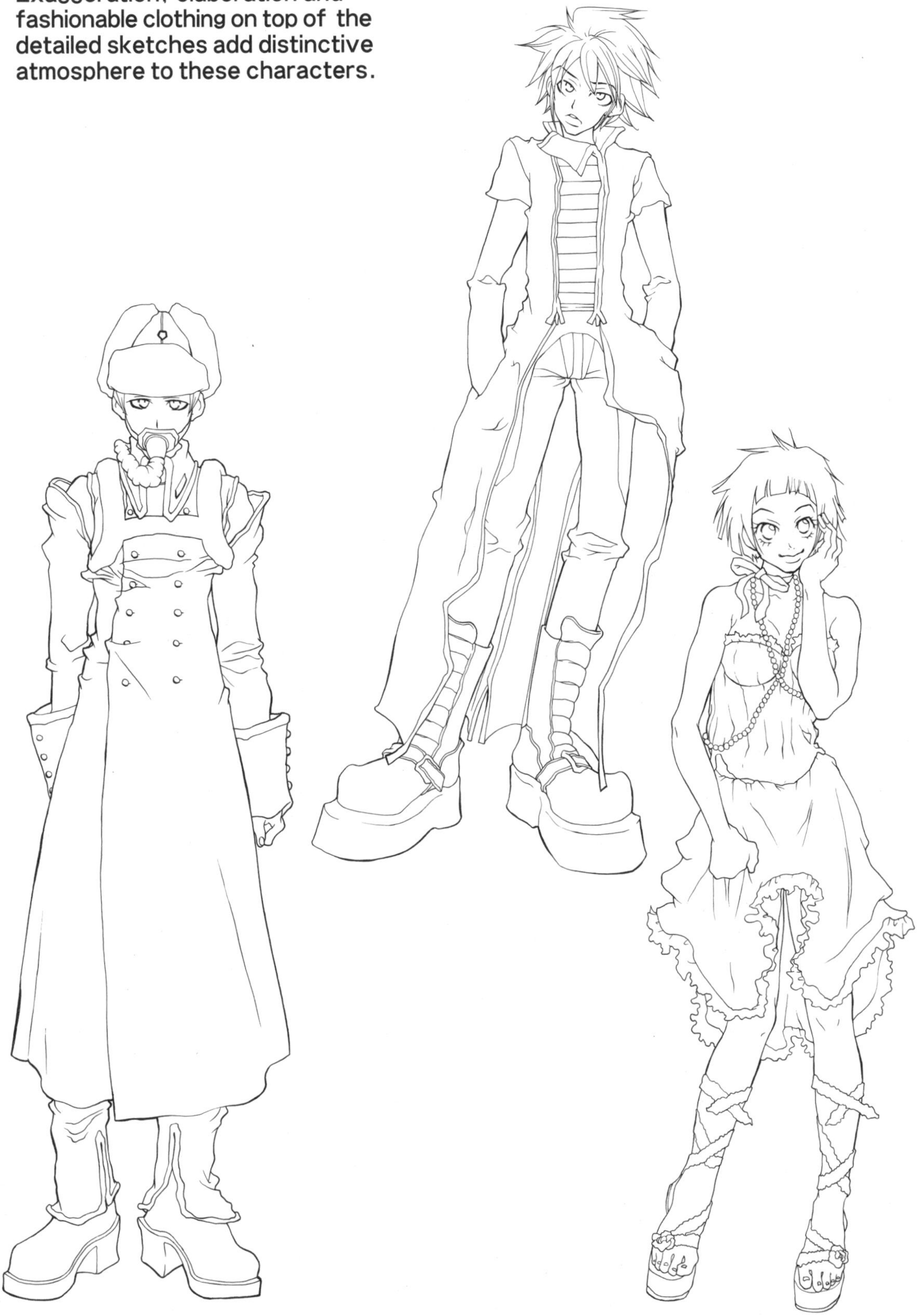

C: Drawing Simplified Anime Style Characters

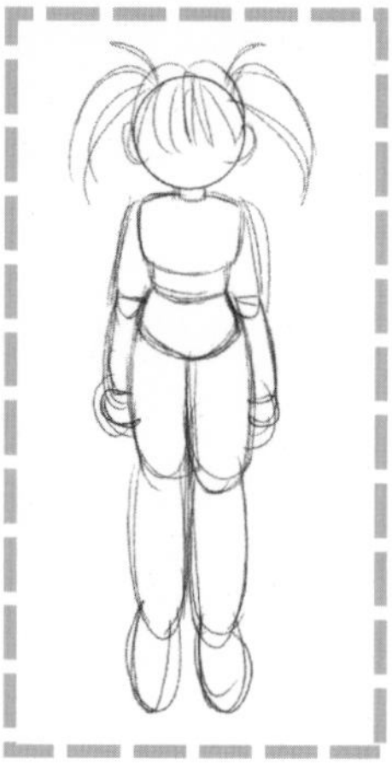

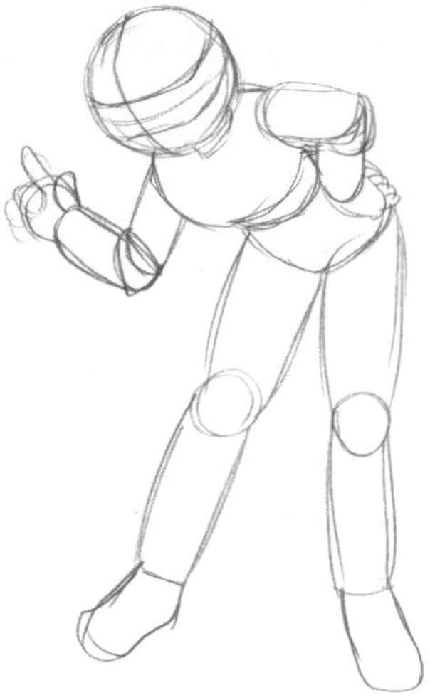

① Use the basic model and decide on a pose.

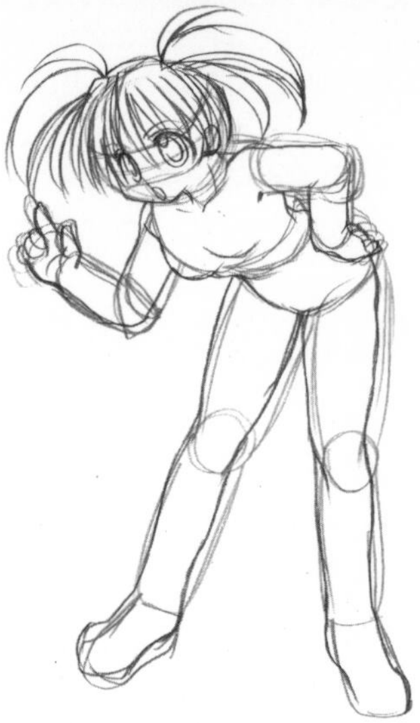

② Build up the body.

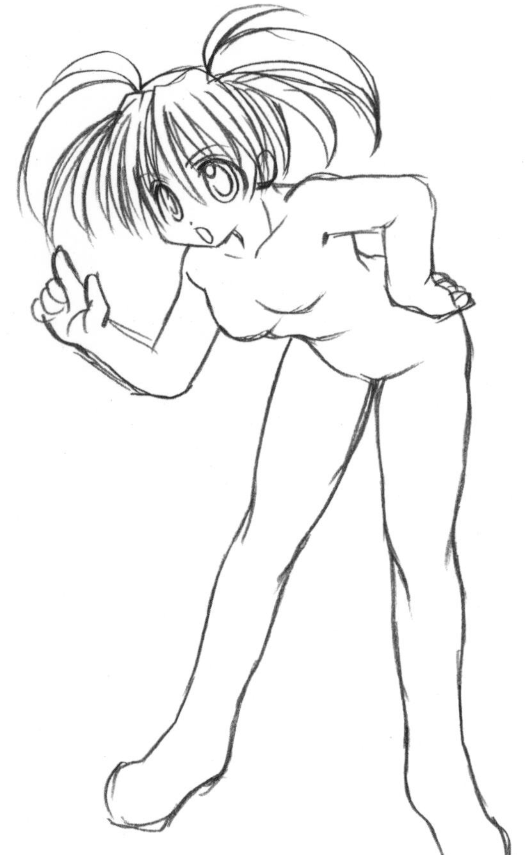

③ Clean up the lines and finish without having the character wear any clothes.

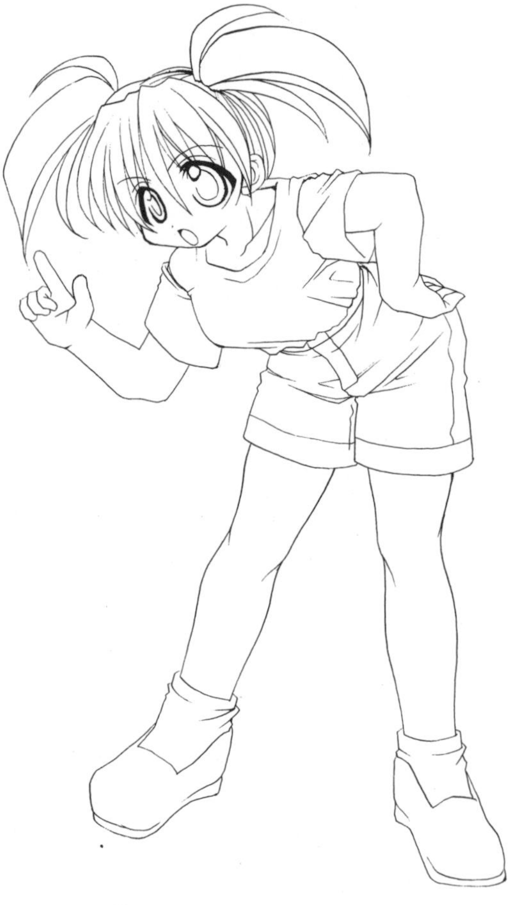

④ Dress the character.

Developing Characters Using Patterns

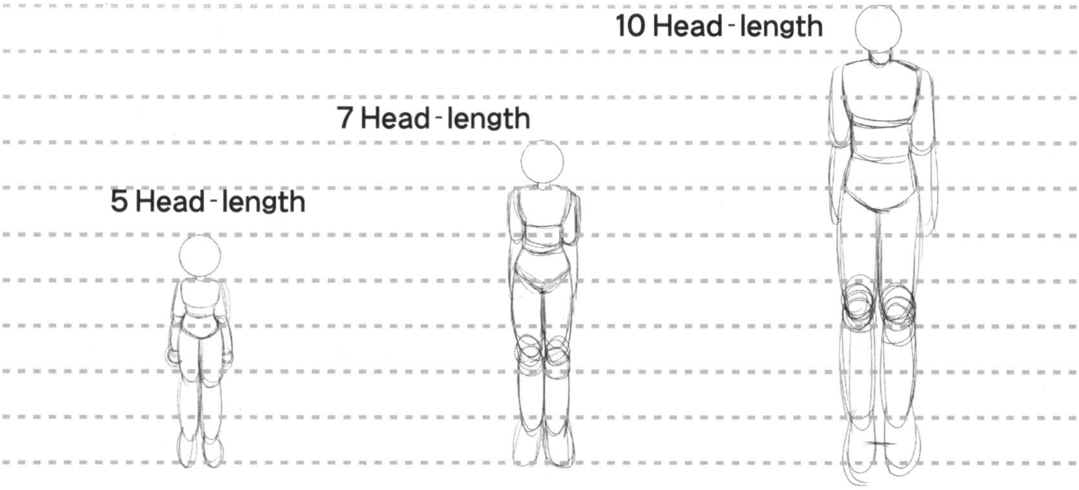
10 Head - length
7 Head - length
5 Head - length

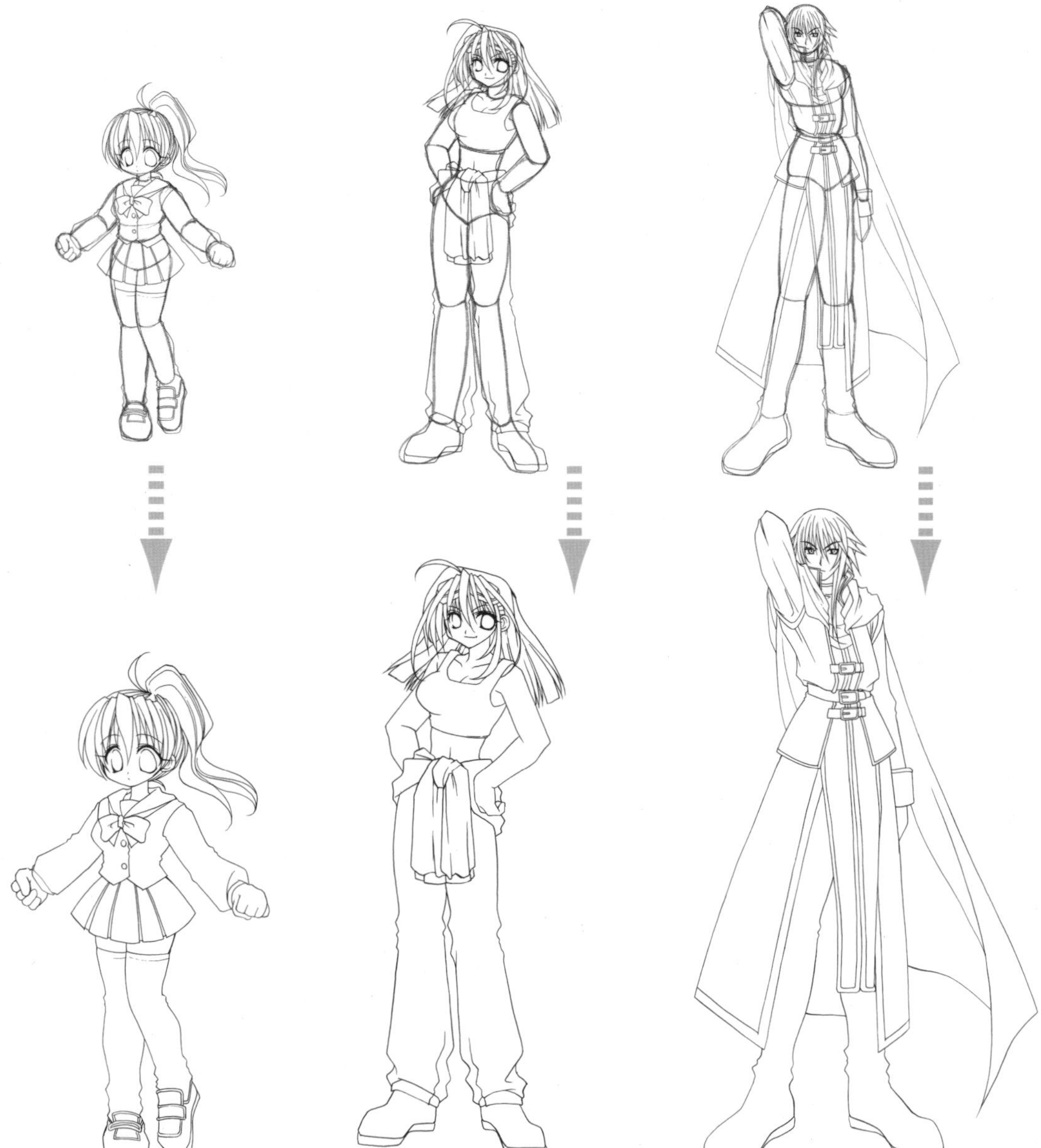

Drawing 5 Head-Lengthed Characters

5 head-length bodies are usually used for creating children or non-human, fairy or hermit characters. Head can remain a circle.

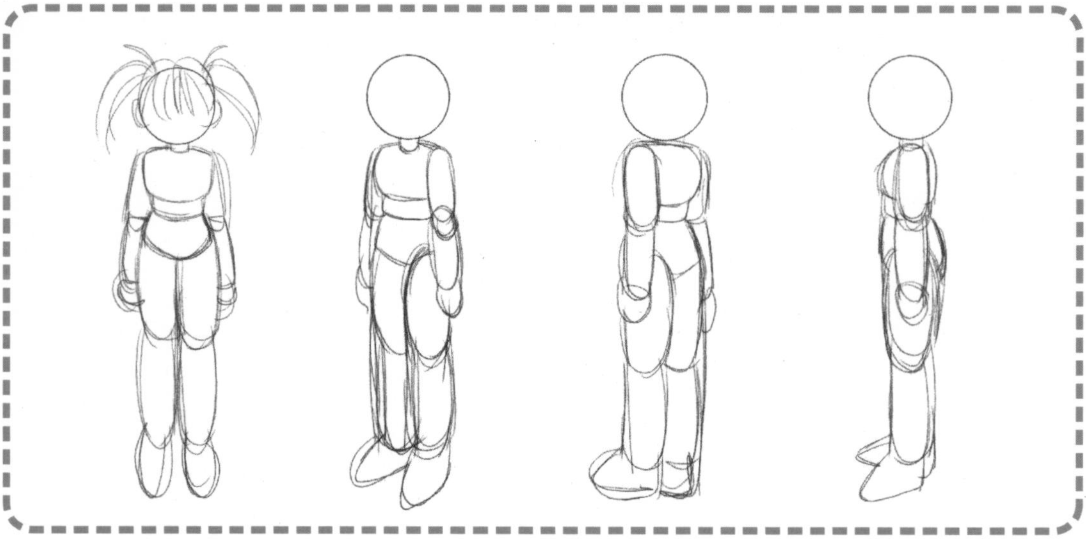

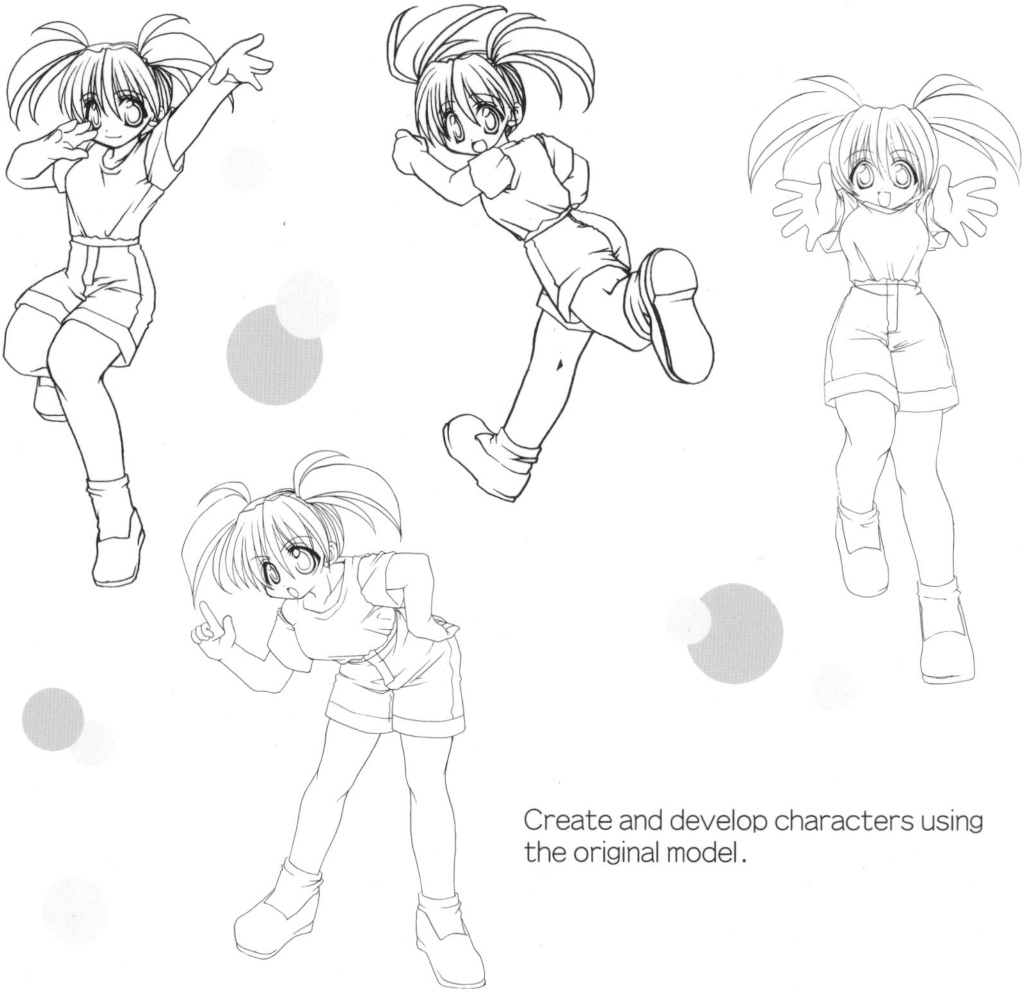

Create and develop characters using the original model.

Drawing 7 Head-Lengthed Characters

7 head length bodies are close to real human bodies and usually used for creating young female or children. Female hero and boy characters are also common. First, draw a genderless model and develop them afterwards.

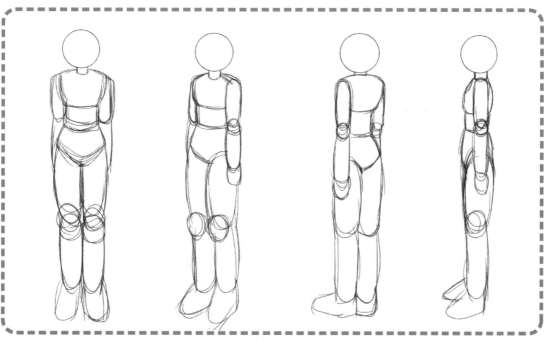

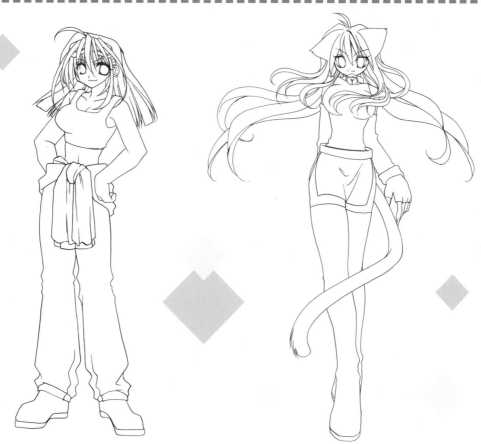

Drawing 10 Head-Lengthed Characters

10 head length bodies are suited for characters with supernatural powers like superheroes or powerful enemies. The emphasis is on the long legs. Be careful with the position of the knees and draw out a model.

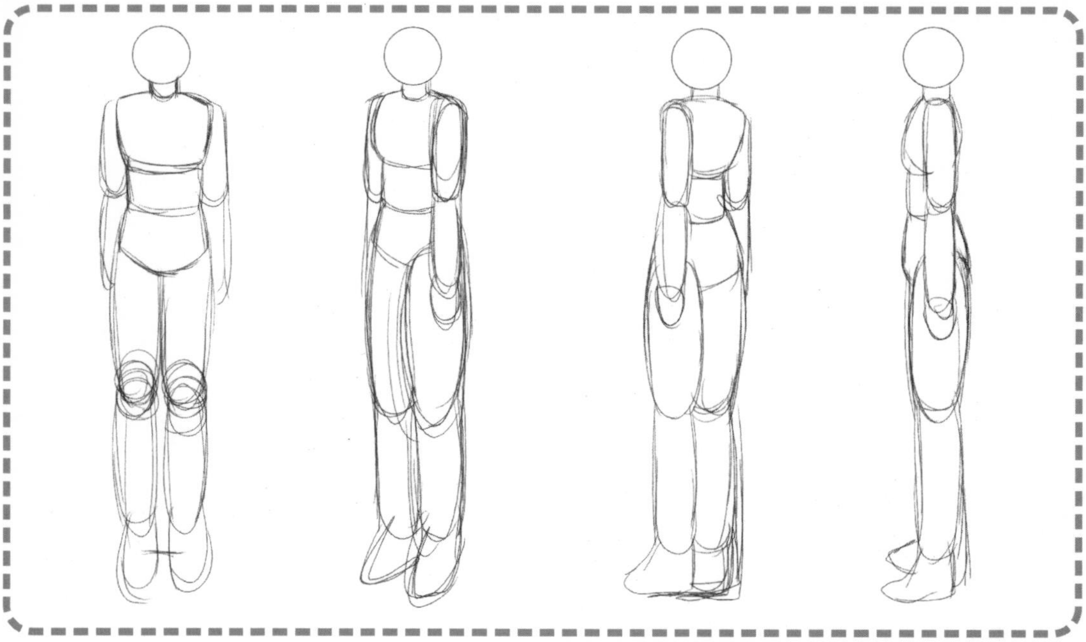

The best way to emphasize the immensity of the 10 head - length body is to have the character stand next to a 5 head - lengthed character.

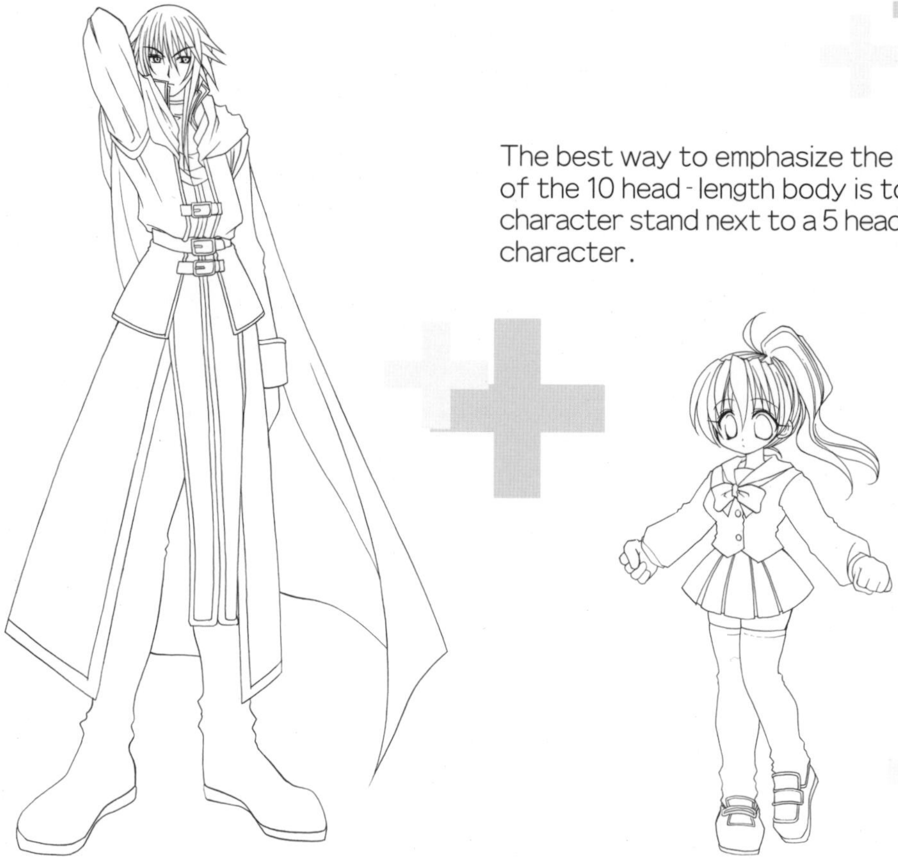

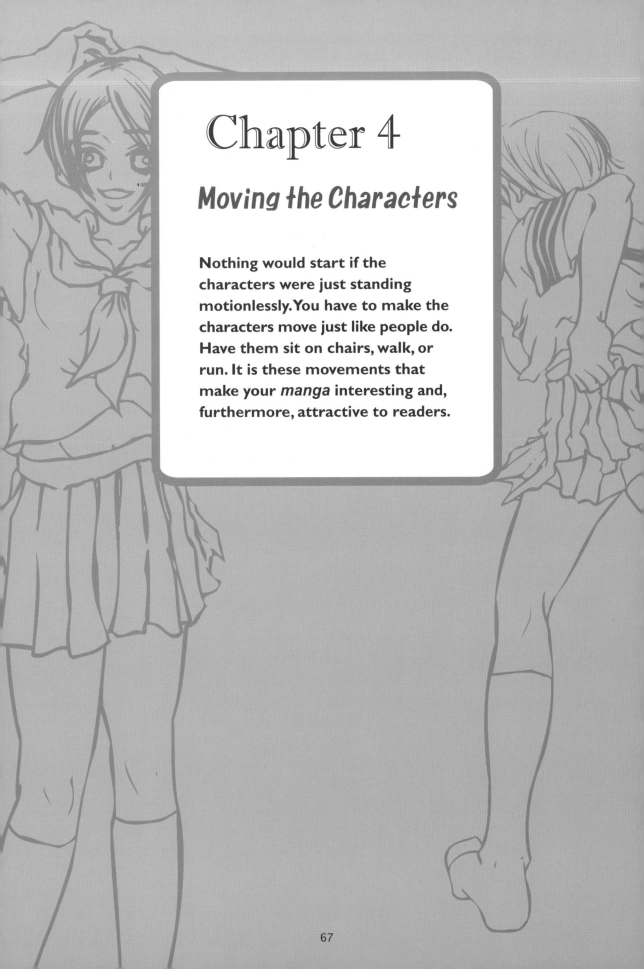

Chapter 4

Moving the Characters

Nothing would start if the characters were just standing motionlessly. You have to make the characters move just like people do. Have them sit on chairs, walk, or run. It is these movements that make your *manga* interesting and, furthermore, attractive to readers.

Sitting Poses 1

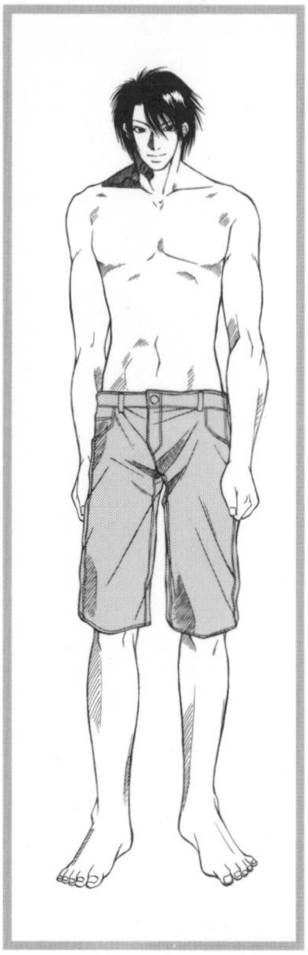

Sketch out an original figure. Develop it to a character sitting down, while being careful of its proportion.

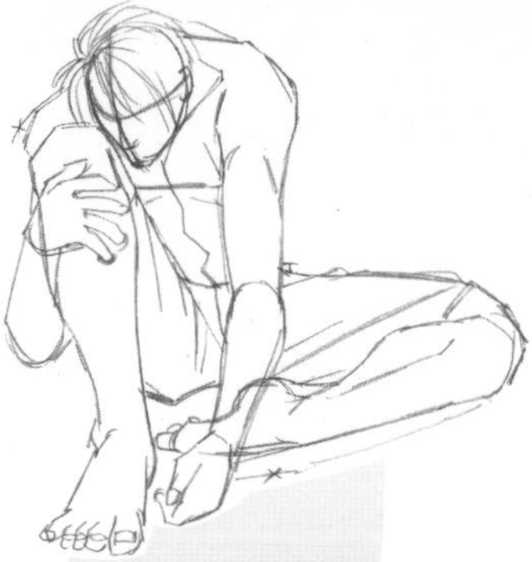

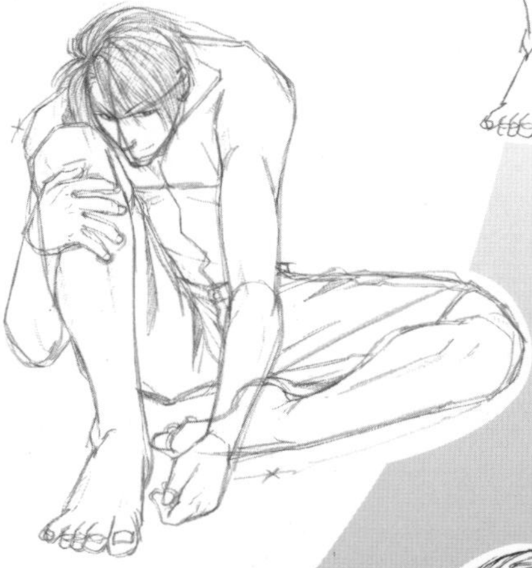

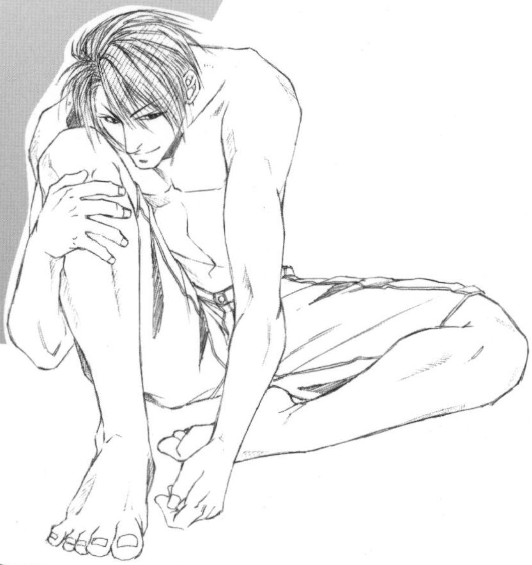

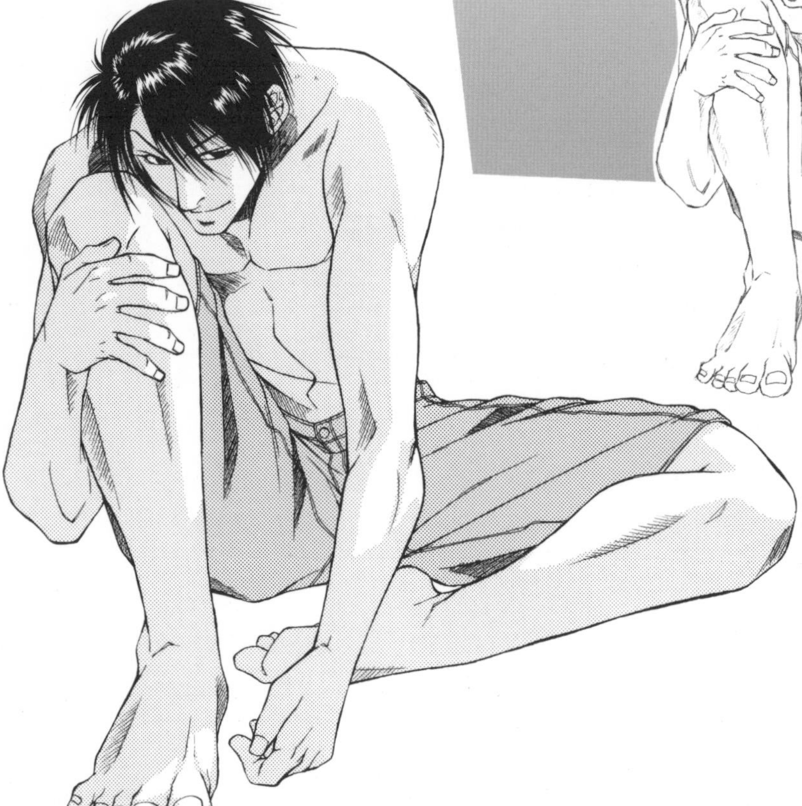

Sitting Poses 2

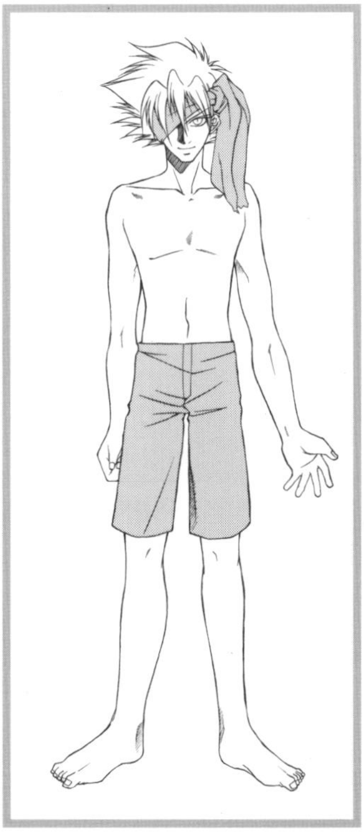

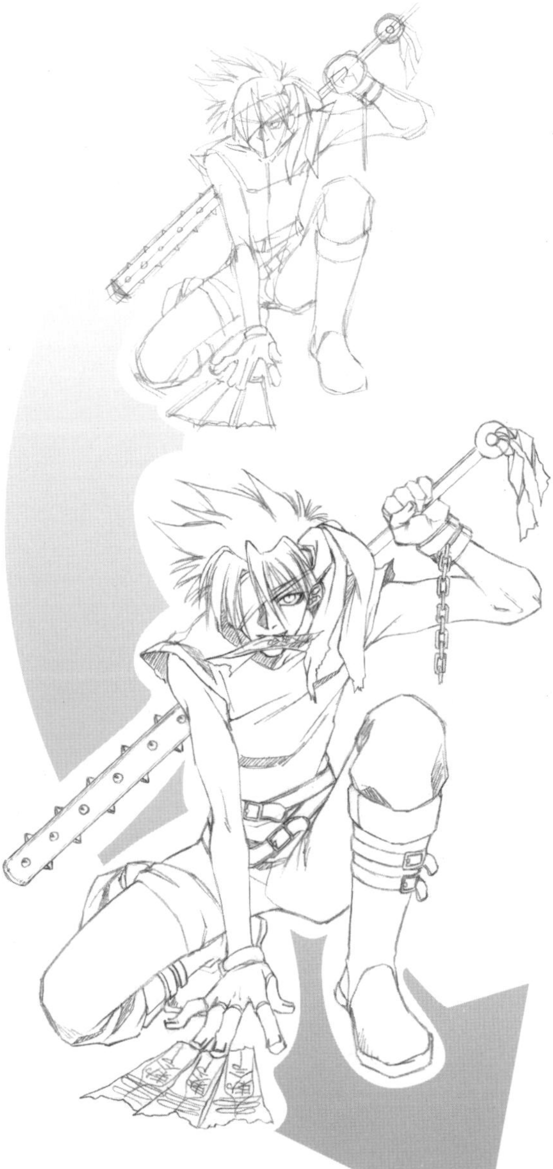

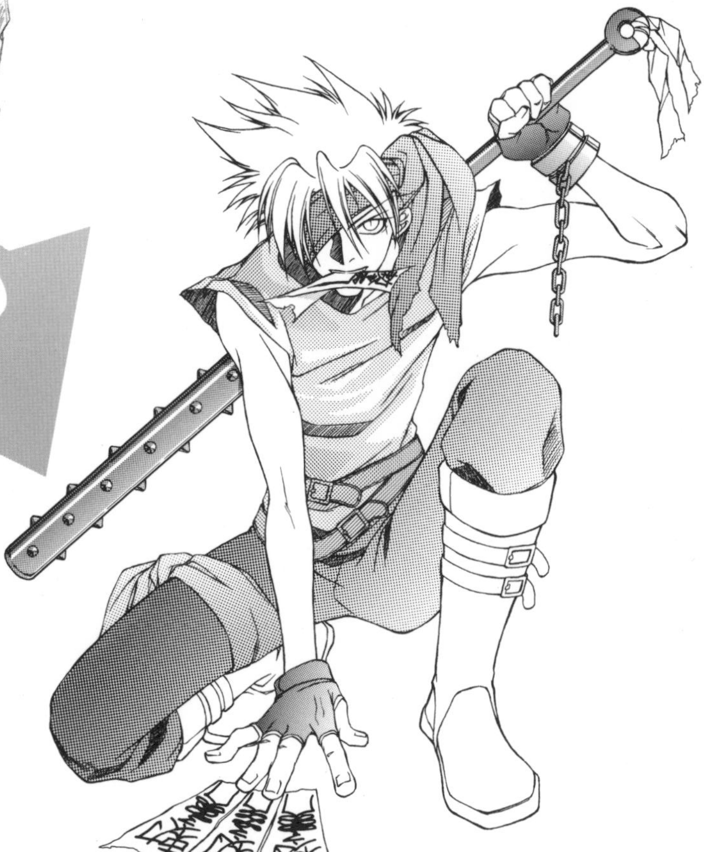

Sitting Poses 3

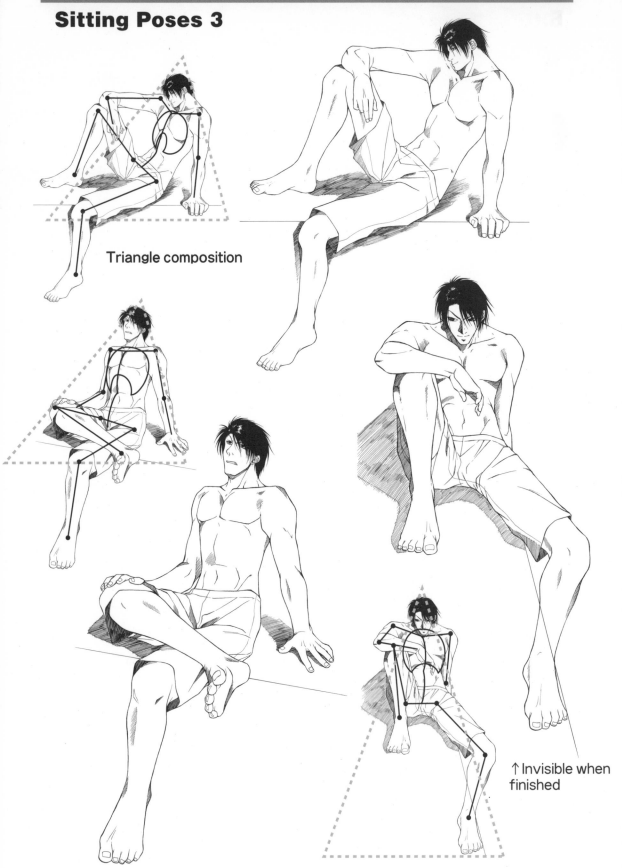

Triangle composition

↑ Invisible when finished

Running Poses

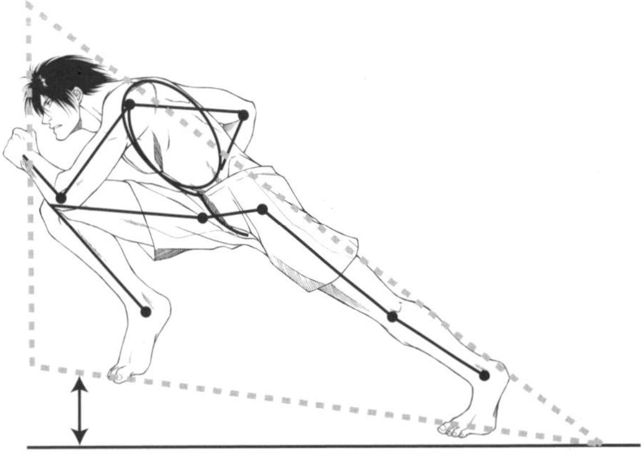

The triangle space between the front foot and the ground makes the character seem very animate.

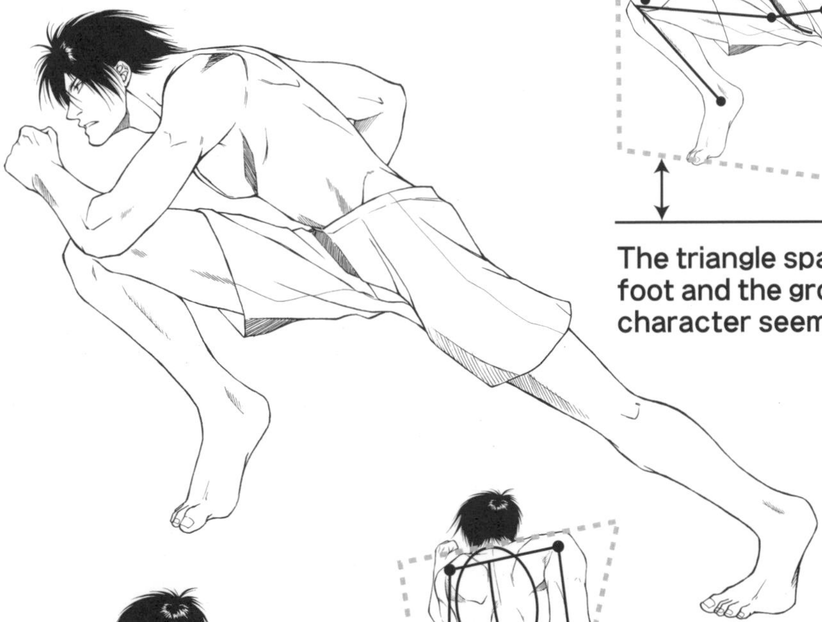

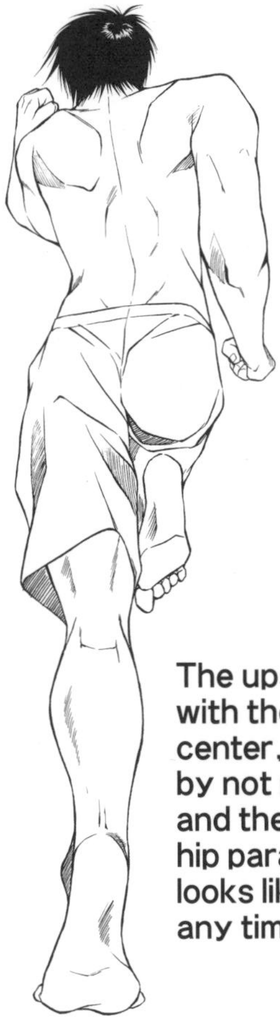

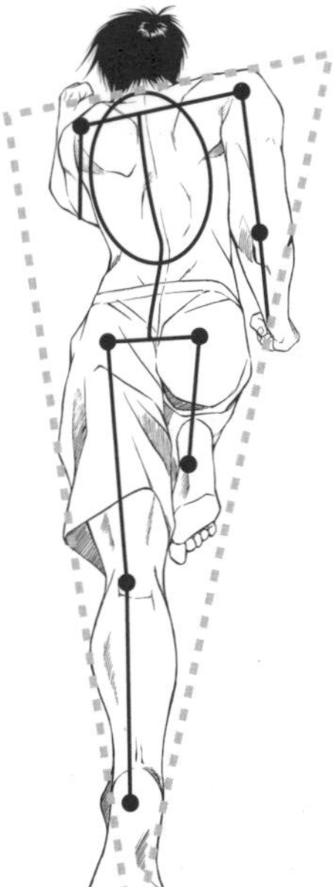

The upside-down triangle, with the back foot in the center, creates motion. And by not making the shoulders and the horizontal line of the hip parallel, the character looks like it can start running any time.

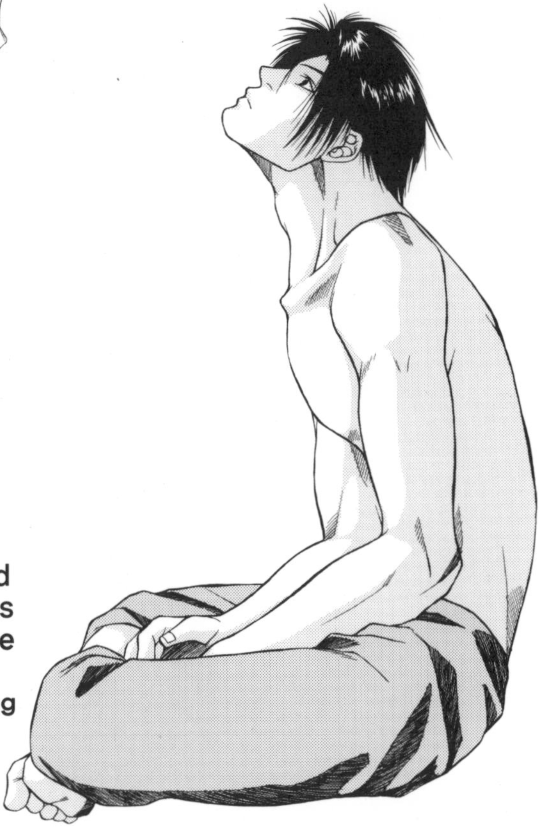

Running Poses

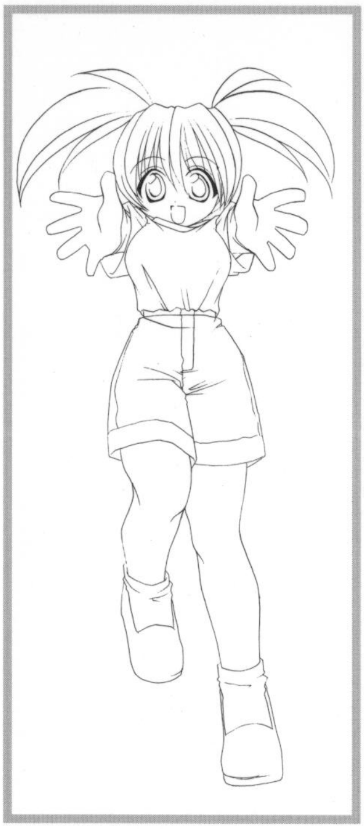

Use the model doll to try out different angles and poses, and practice on creating a scene full of movements.

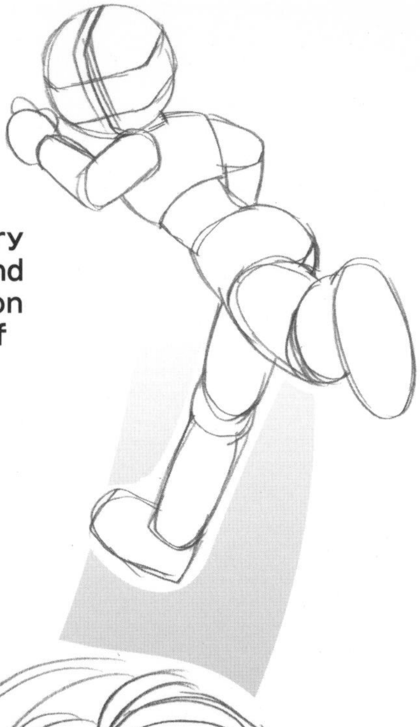

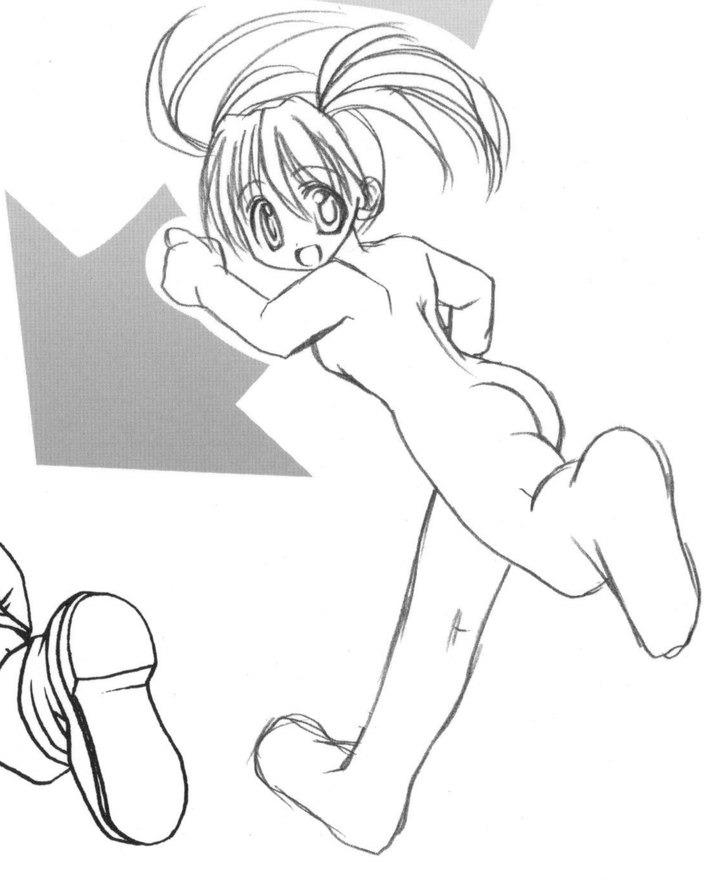

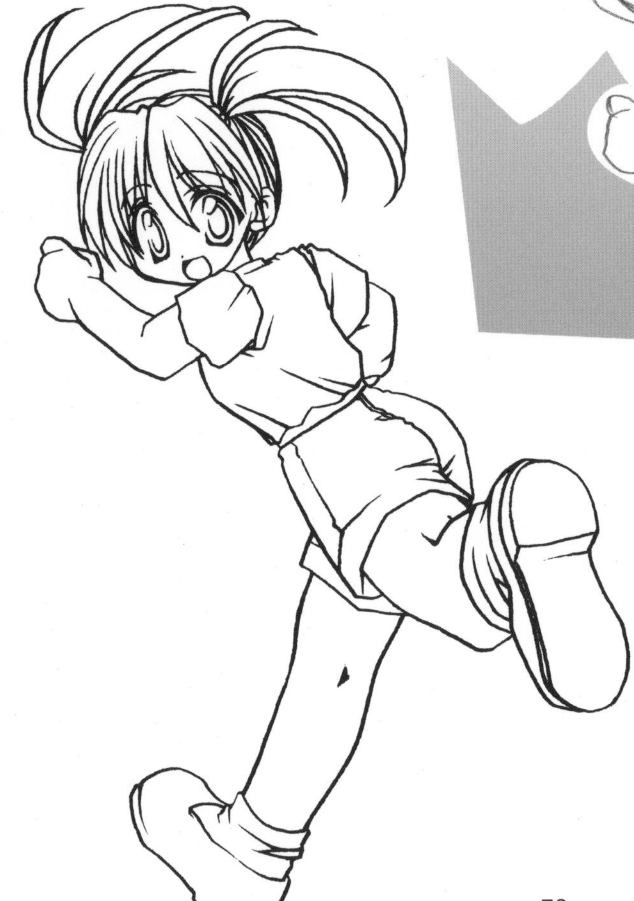

Miscellaneous Poses

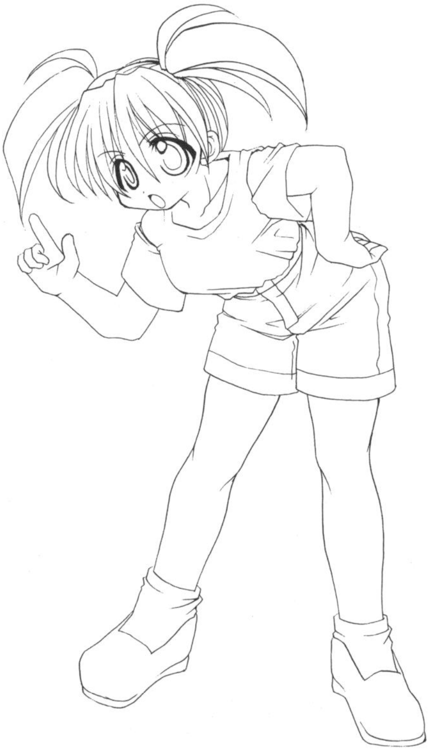

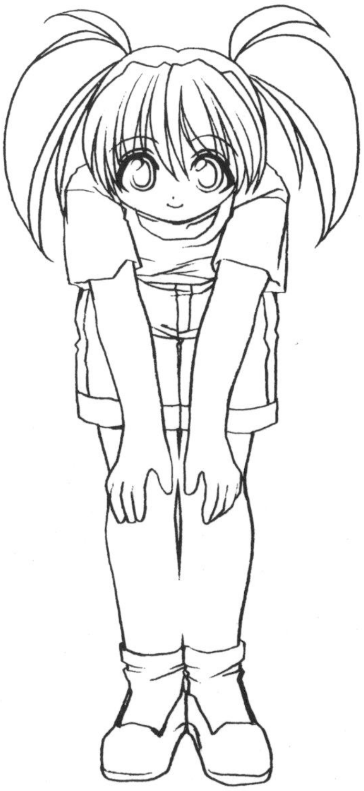

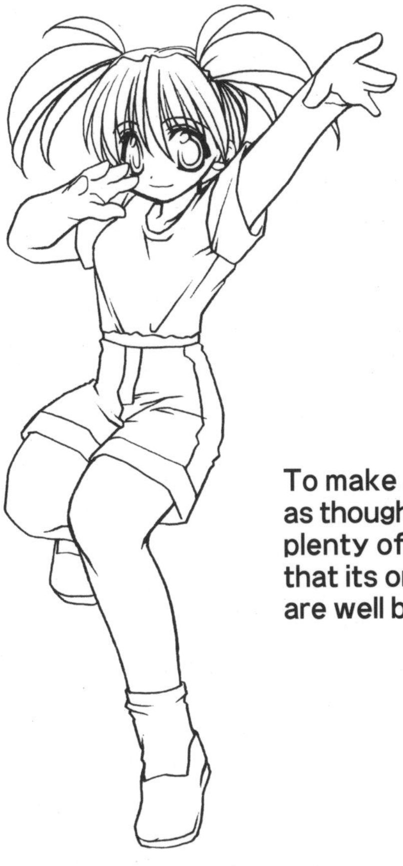

To make a character look as though it is dancing with plenty of action, it is vital that its original sketches are well balanced.

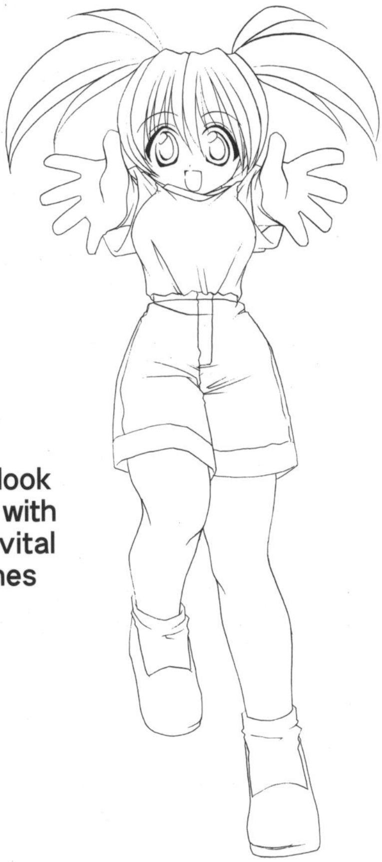

Miscellaneous Poses

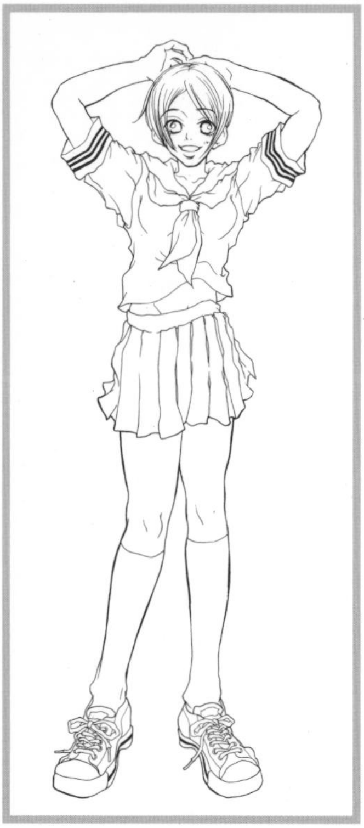

Practice drawing a single character posing differently in many angles. Before you know it, you will be able to create scenes easily.

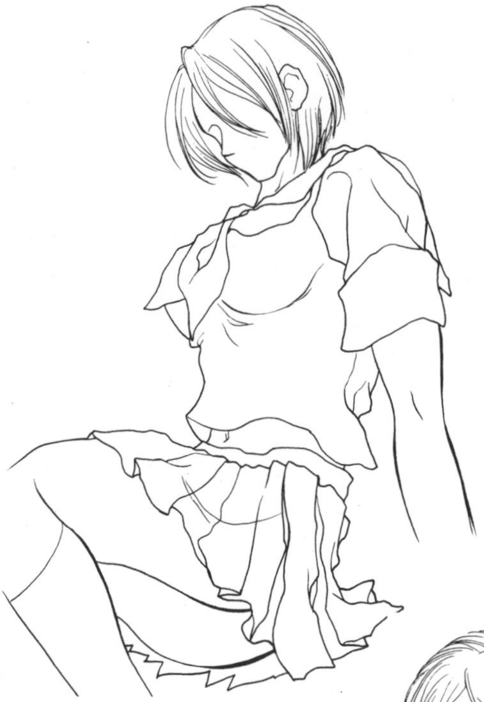

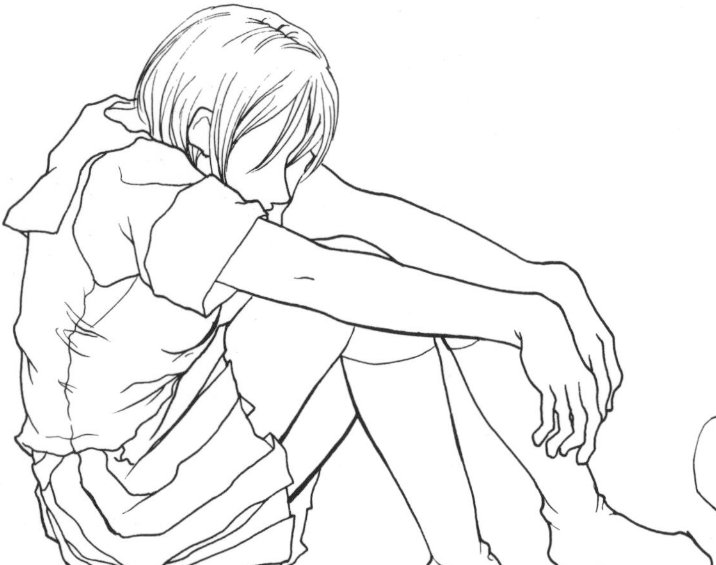

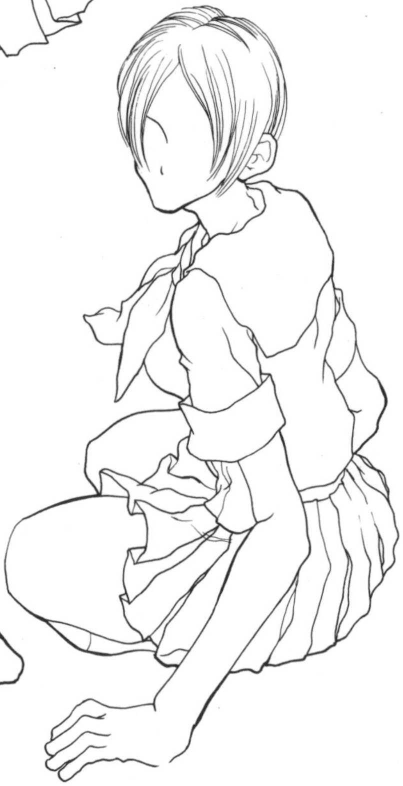

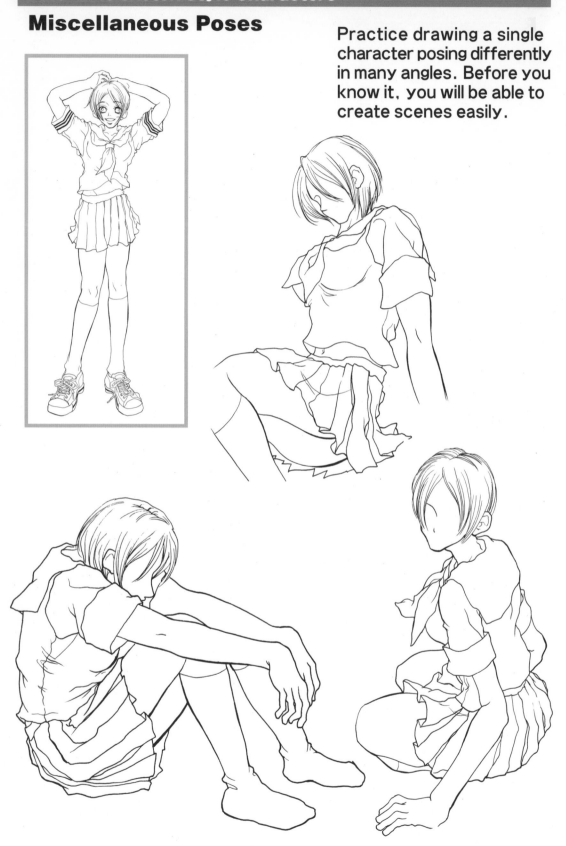

Running Poses

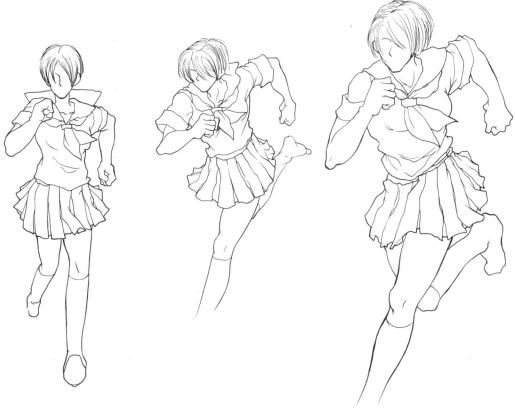

When drawing a moving character, be sure to add such details as creases in their clothing and movements of hair. Make them look animate and full of life.

Leg and Back Poses

Downward Angle

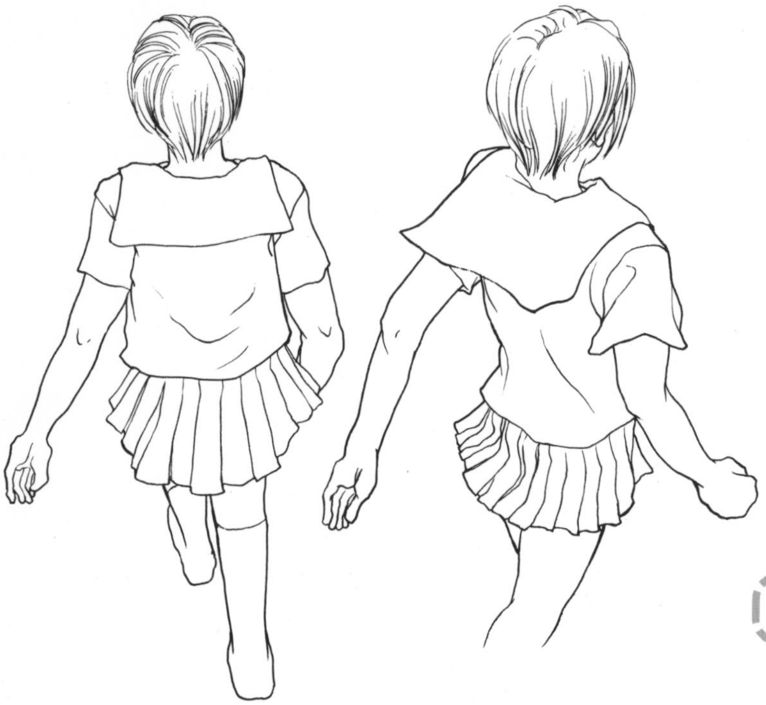

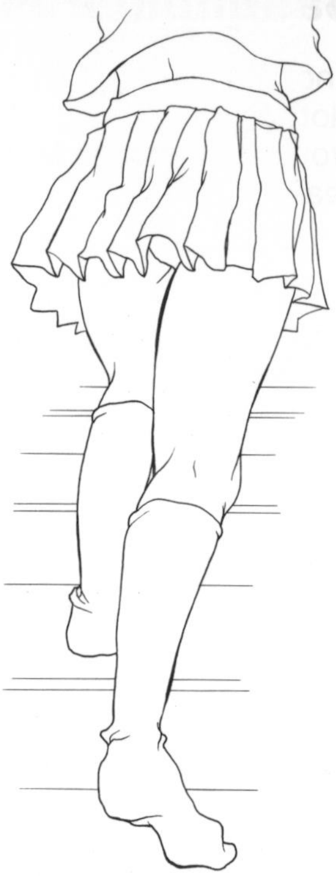

Upward Angle

Position of legs when sitting down

For creating under-the-table scenes.

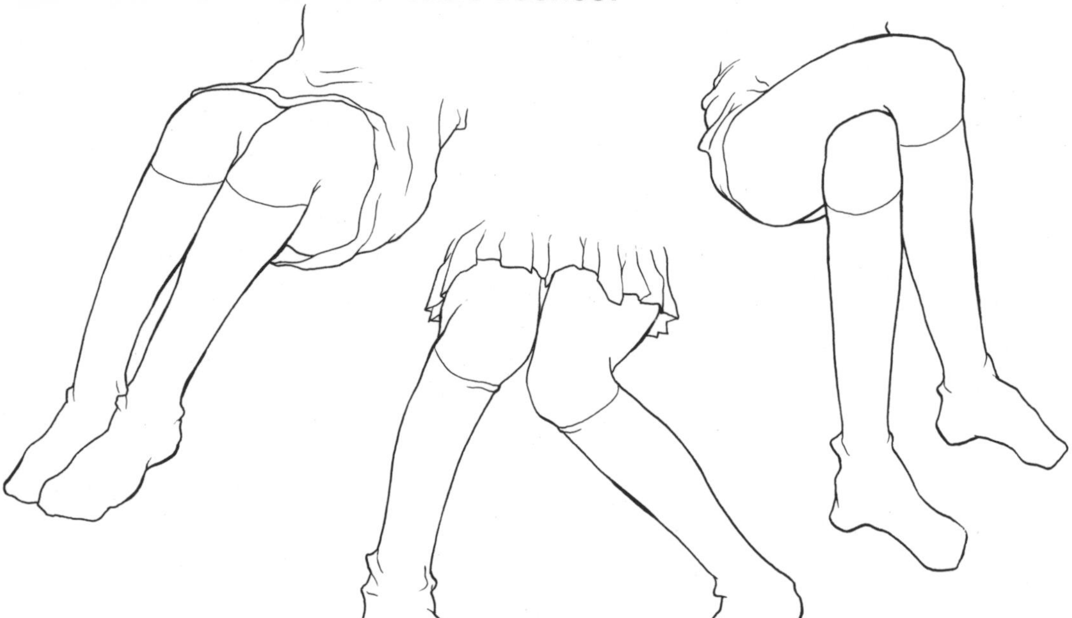

Samples of Putting in Outlines

Knowing how to draw characters without their clothes on (either nude or with underwear) would help you express the characters more realistically.

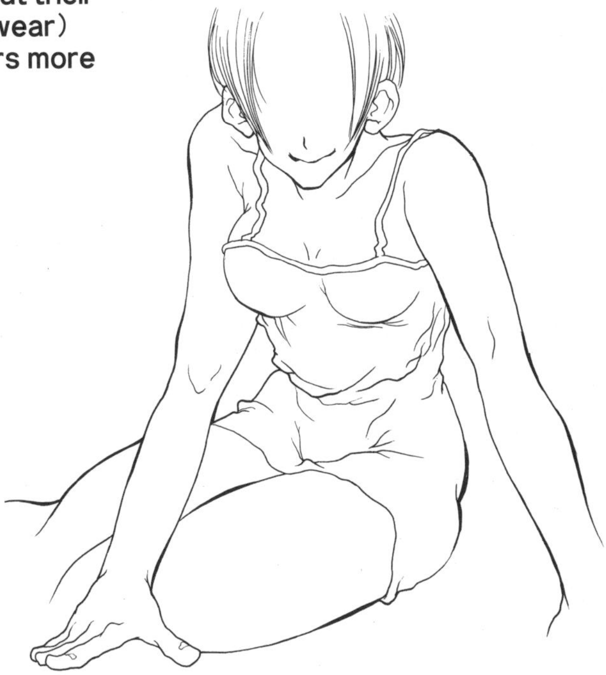

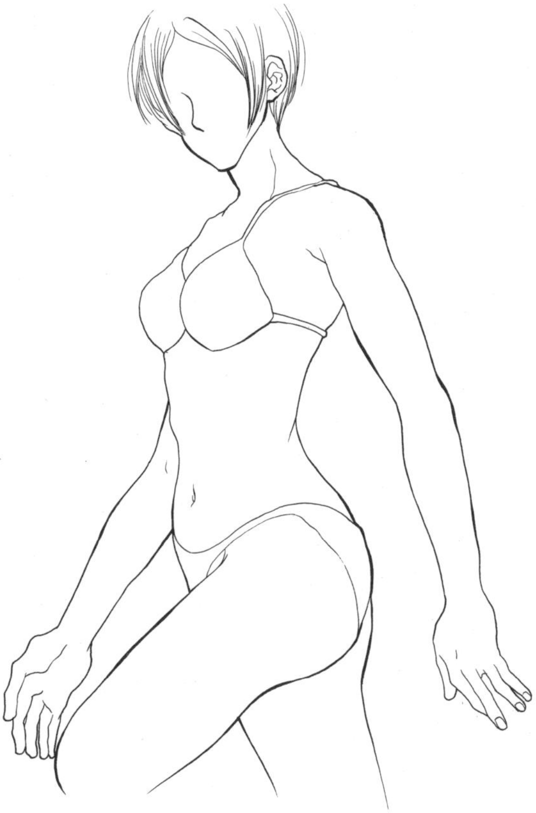

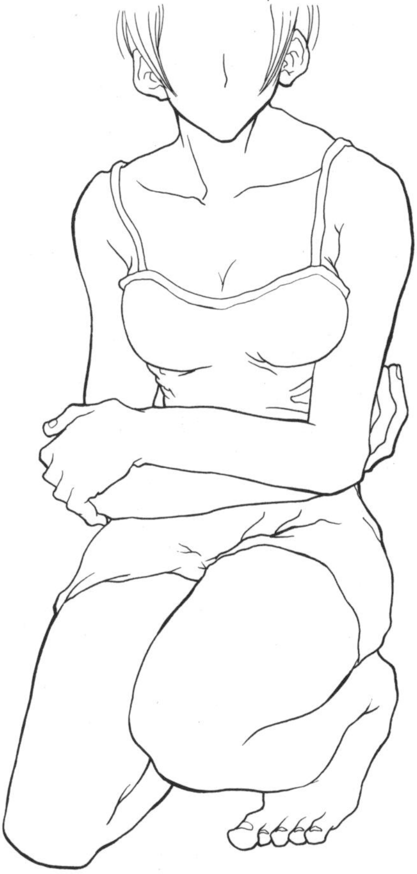

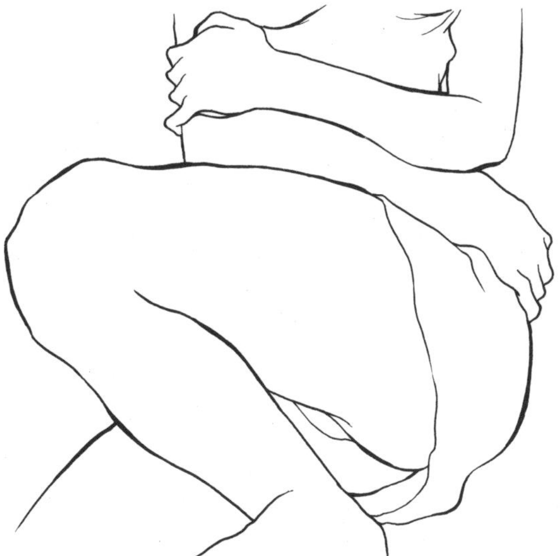

Samples

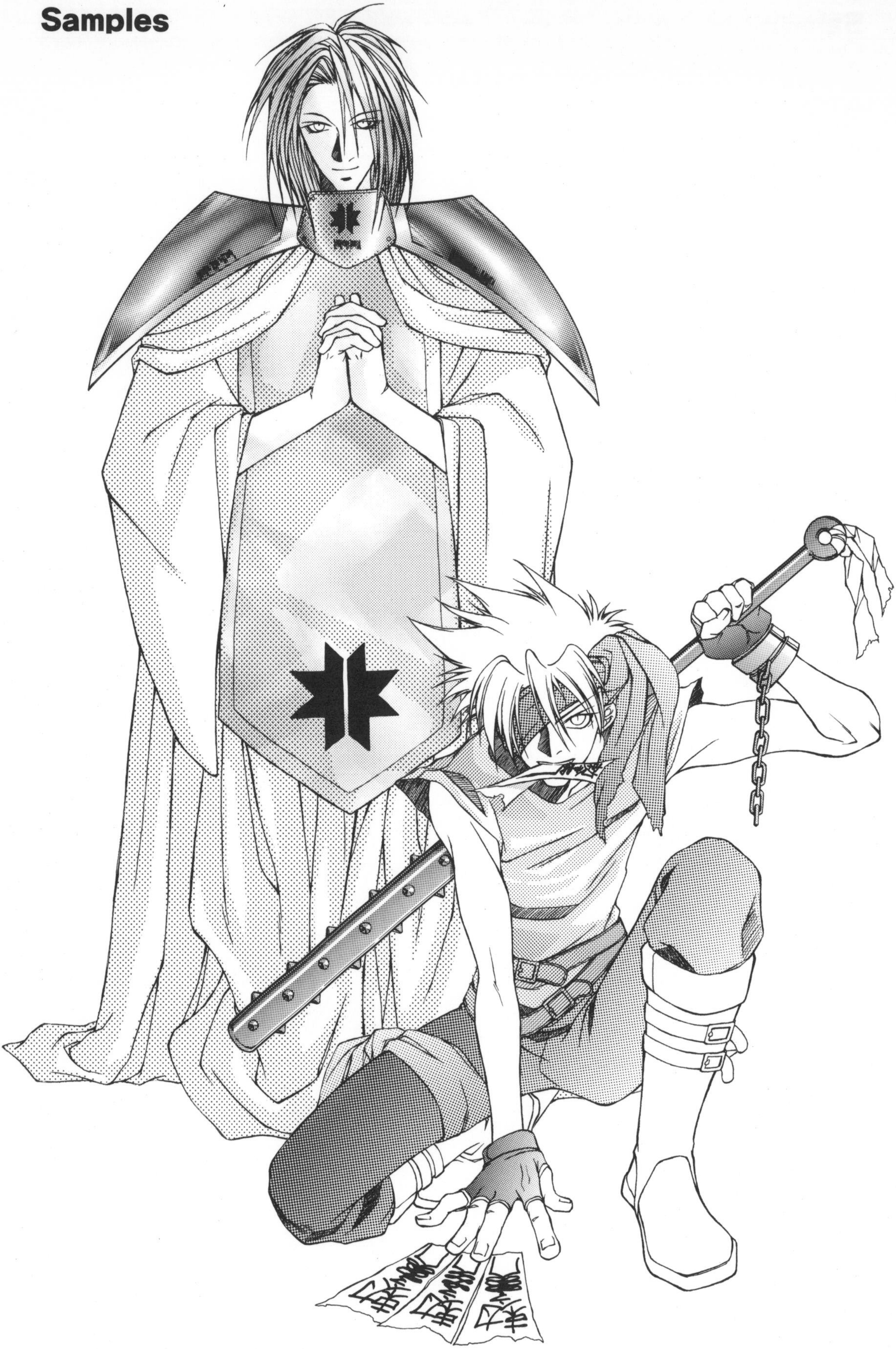

Samples

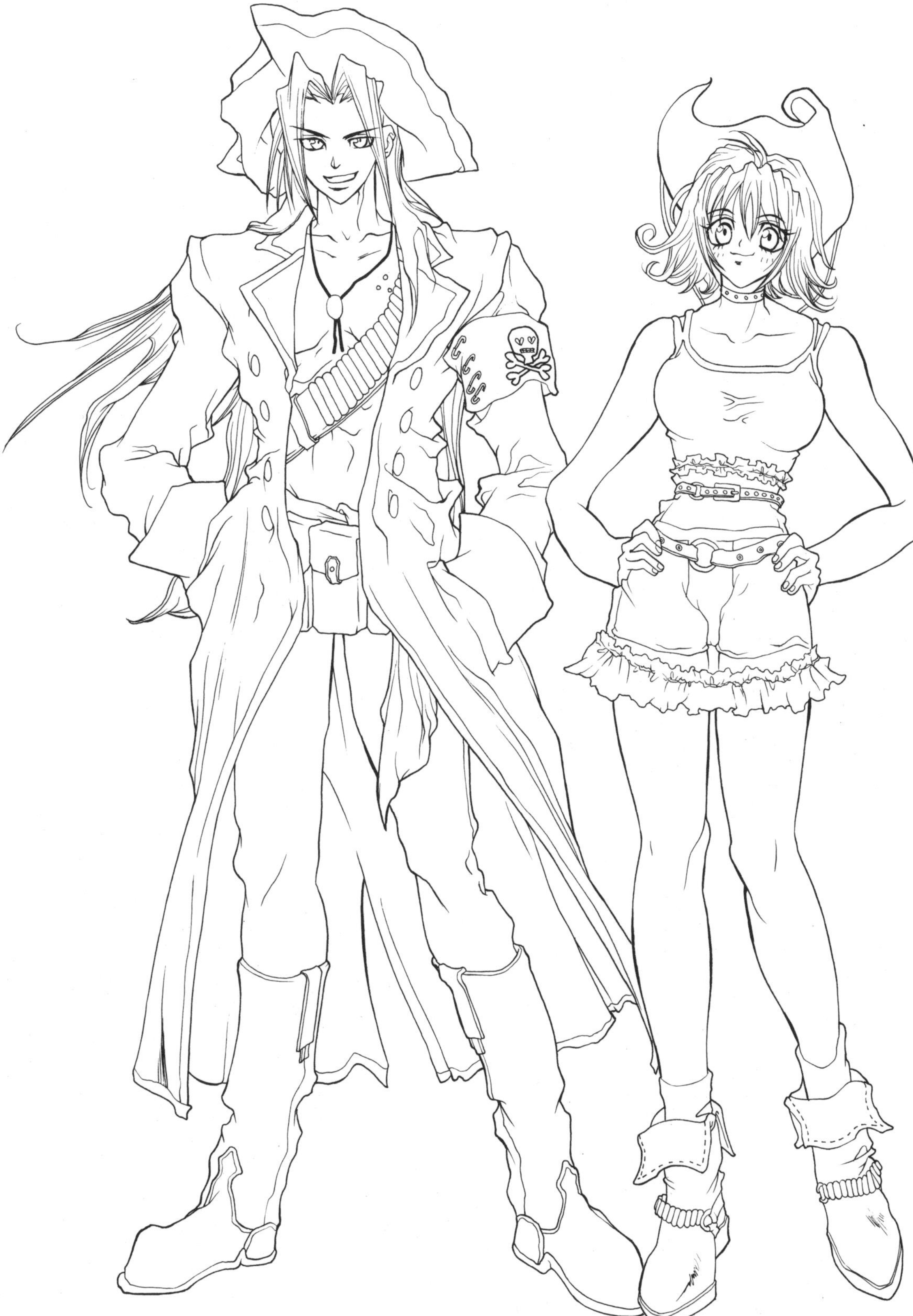

Samples

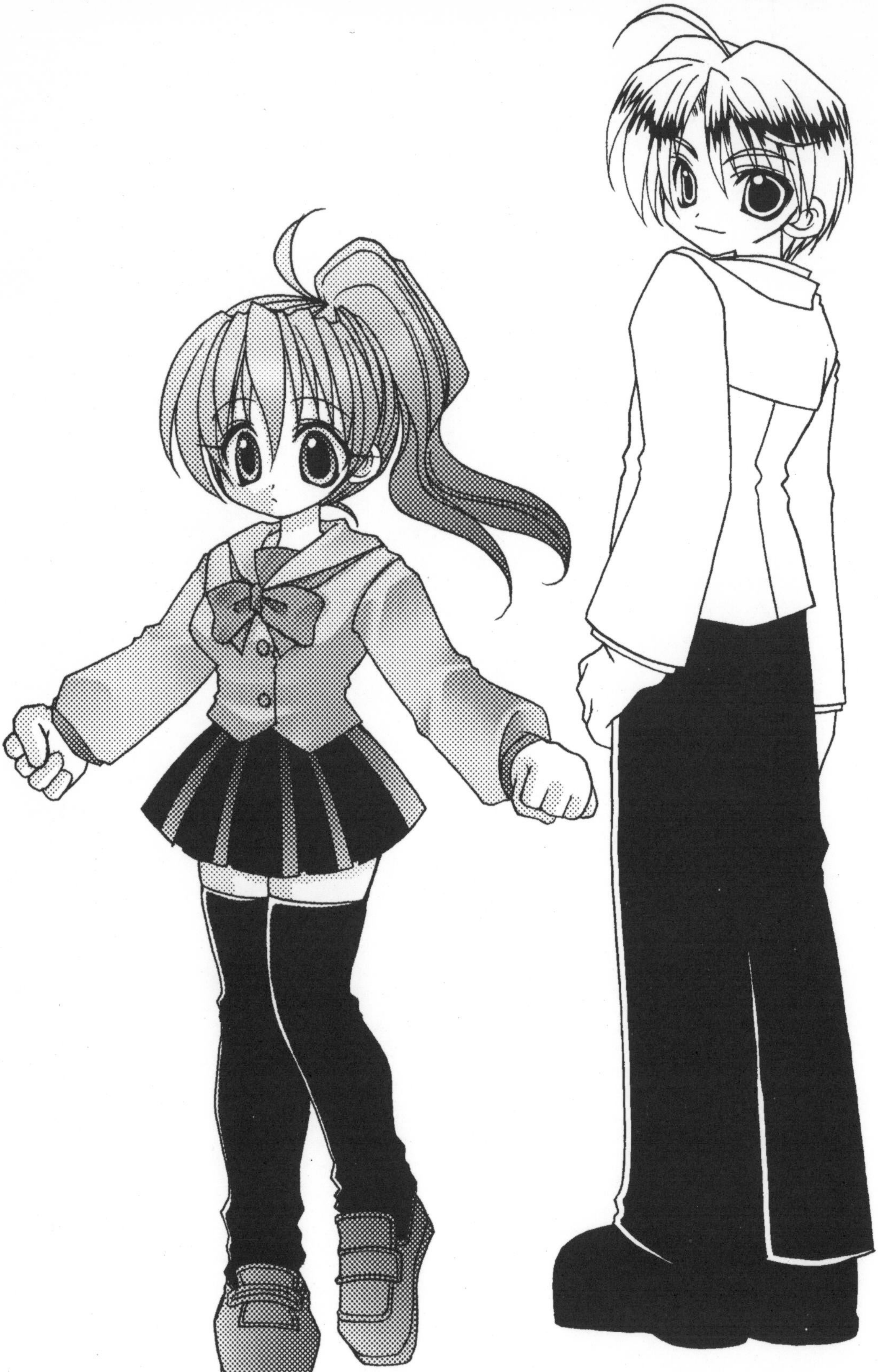